The Alcoholics Anonymous Experience

The Alcoholics

A CLOSE-UP VIEW

Anonymous Experience

FOR PROFESSIONALS

Milton A. Maxwell, Ph.D.

McGRAW-HILL BOOK COMPANY

New York • St. Louis • San Francisco
Auckland • Bogotá • Hamburg • Johannesburg • London
Madrid • Mexico • Montreal • New Delhi • Panama • Paris • São Paulo
Singapore • Sydney • Tokyo • Toronto

Thomas H. Quinn and Michael Hennelly were the editors of this book. Christopher Simon was the designer. Teresa F. Leaden supervised the production. It was set in Times Roman by *Byrd*.

Printed and bound by The Book Press, Inc.

LIBRARY OF CONGRESS CATALOGING IN PUBLICATION DATA

Maxwell, Milton A.
    The Alcoholics Anonymous experience.

    Bibliography: p.
    Includes index.
    1. Alcoholics Anonymous.   2. Social work with alcoholics.   I. Title
    HV5287.A48M39 1984   362.2′9286   83-16244
    ISBN 0-07-040996-X

1 2 3 4 5 6 7 8 9 0 BKP BKP 8 9 8 7 6 5 4

ISBN 0-07-040996-X

Contents

Preface

Because my goal in this book is a reliable and insightful description of the personal and collective aspects of Alcoholics Anonymous, the reader has a right to know something about the road I have traveled in arriving at my comprehension of both alcoholism and A.A.

The critical experience setting me on this course was my doctoral dissertation on social factors in the Alcoholics Anonymous program (1949). I am not an alcoholic (nor abstainer), and I had no particular interest in either alcoholism or A.A. It was my interest in the interpersonal theories of personality development and change—in the traditions of Charles Horton Cooley, George Herbert Mead, Harry Stack Sullivan, and Karen Horney—which led to my research focus on the still-young phenomenon of A.A.

I knew only one A.A. member, but fortunately he had the interest and influence to persuade his Chicago suburban A.A. group of about 20 regular attenders to let me be a participant observer for a summer. The members soon trusted me, and I participated in every type of activity, in and outside of the meetings. I was not only able to observe the full range of A.A. interaction at close range, but I gained a feeling for what was happening. In fact, I experienced some change in myself. So, I ended the summer with keen awareness of the potency of an A.A.-type of intimate, honest peer group.

Then, through a chain of contacts begun in this group, I obtained systematic data on selected aspects of the recovery experiences of 150 A.A. members located in seven states and four Canadian provinces. Analyzing and trying to make theoretical sense of the two sets of experiences was engrossing and enlightening—not only with regard to understanding A.A. but also understanding the nature and etiology of alcoholism.

However, as much as I learned, this was only the beginning. The process of gaining a more inclusive perspective on alcoholism and A.A. was furthered by attending the pioneer Yale Summer School of Alcohol Studies. This was followed by undergraduate and graduate teaching: not only on alcoholism but also on group dynamics and on personality in relation to culture and social structure. My understanding of personality change was also enhanced by psychotherapeutic perspectives.

The expansion of my perspective on alcoholism and the recovery process was also furthered by contacts with many alcoholics who were not in A.A.—chiefly while I was doing research on patients in a nationally known private hospital for alcoholics (1958), while doing research on Skid Row alcoholics (with Peterson, 1958), and on a broad spectrum of alcoholic employees (1960, 1972).

Over the years, I have also had extensive opportunities to look at alcoholism and A.A. through the eyes of all types of professional persons. While at Washington State University, I served a dozen years on the advisory committee of the state's alcoholism program. I also spent a year as a staff member of the alcoholism program of Alberta.

In 1965, I was invited to Rutgers University as Professor of Sociology at the Center of Alcohol Studies and Executive Director of the Rutgers Summer School of Alcohol Studies. This affiliation greatly multiplied my contacts with professional helpers and scientists from all over North America and from overseas.

The location also led to unusual opportunities to become very familiar with the structure and operations of A.A. as a whole. One of these opportunities was the time and support to undertake a fresh study of A.A.

The major goal of the new study was to obtain the necessary data for an up-to-date portrayal of A.A. operations and dynamics, with particular attention to the personal-participation experiences of members and the dynamics of local group life. The approach was essentially anthropological—that of both participant observation and the use of knowledgeable informants. The scope was comprehensive, including all the major varieties of group and individual patterns.

The taped interviews with individual members regarding their own experiences before and after coming into A.A. became the source of most of the excerpts which are featured throughout the book.

Needless to say, gathering, processing, and assimilating this material gave me a still more complete view of A.A. phenomena. But this is not all. I also gained a still more comprehensive perspective on the nature of alcoholism and its development— a greater feeling for what alcoholics go through in becoming alcoholic. And, I also gained a greater awareness of the basic and profound changes which so many A.A. members undergo in the process of recovering.

I also became even more conscious of how elusive a *full* understanding is of the phenomenon we call Alcoholics Anonymous. It would take volumes to present all interpretative possibilities. Yet I have obtained a close enough view of A.A. to feel obligated to communicate what I have learned.

I should hasten to add that the book is no substitute for personal contacts with A.A. members and groups. However, the book can serve as a time-saving introduction or supplement. Hopefully, it will also sensitize the reader to some of the less obvious facets of the total Alcoholics Anonymous experience.

Acknowledgments

First of all, I wish to acknowledge my great indebtedness to L.E.S. who, in 1947, initially opened a window for me to Alcoholics Anonymous—to his own experience, his home group, and to the larger A.A. society.

I also wish to thank the many other A.A. members who, then and over the years, have contributed to my knowledge about A.A. and understanding its dynamics.

Further, I am indebted to all who participated in my more recent study of A.A., and for the grant which gave me the time to concentrate on it. (NIAAA Grant No. 5 R18 AA00487) Joan K. Jackson was my chief consultant throughout, serving as research adviser and, during the later bookwriting, also giving me the benefit of her professional judgment and editorial counsel. Daniel J. Anderson also made his rich experience available as research consultant.

Central to the study was the field work, so much of which was done by J.M., H.M. and E.S. I am thankful to them for the care and skill they exercised as observers and interviewers, and for the insights they and their respondents contributed.

Also, I am grateful to Marjorie L. Dreher who was deeply

involved in the study, from start to finish. In multiple ways, she competently and conscientiously fulfilled her roles as secretary and research assistant.

Finally, I want to express my great appreciation to my wife, Charlotte, for her interest in the project and for her unwavering moral support.

THE PREAMBLE

*Alcoholics Anonymous is a fellowship of men
and women who share their experience,
strength and hope with each other that they
may solve their common problem and
help others to recover from alcoholism.*

*The only requirement for membership is a
desire to stop drinking. There are no dues or
fees for A.A. membership; we are self-
supporting through our own contributions.
A.A. is not allied with any sect, denomination,
politics, organization or institution;
does not wish to engage in any controversy,
neither endorses nor opposes any causes.
Our primary purpose is to stay sober and
help other alcoholics to achieve sobriety.*

The Alcoholics Anonymous Experience

ONE
Professionals and Alcoholics Anonymous

This book is addressed primarily to all types of professional men and women who have some occasion to deal with alcoholic persons. The goal is to offer them—and other interested persons—an intimate, dependable, and useful portrayal of the personal and collective aspects of the Alcoholics Anonymous experience.

Alcoholics Anonymous has been and continues to be a central phenomenon in the modern alcoholism field. This could not have been predicted at the outset. Many new social phenomena flourish for a time and then fade away. Few survive their founders. Certainly, such a loosely knit fellowship of "alcoholics for alcoholics" would seem to have been a most unlikely candidate for surviving at all. But it has.

Moreover, A.A. has continued to prosper and grow. At first, A.A. was quite alone, for there were few facilities for alcoholics. There was little professional interest in alcoholics or their

1

problem. However, with the increase of professionally directed alcoholism programs and treatment facilities in the 1950s and 1960s, and particularly since 1970, A.A. instead of being displaced has grown more than ever. A.A. groups are now found almost everywhere in the United States and Canada, even in small communities.

A.A. does not keep individual membership records, but it does keep a record of the groups which register (not all do) with the General Service Office in New York. By 1983, they showed that there were over 30,000 groups in these two countries, including over 900 groups in treatment facilities and over 1,100 groups in correctional facilities.

Al-Anon Family Groups, a very similar but totally separate fellowship for spouses, family members, and friends of alcoholics (whether the latter are in A.A. or not) has also experienced rapid growth. By 1983, there were over 20,000 groups worldwide, including over 2,400 Alateen groups for children of alcoholics.

Matthew Dumont (1974) has suggested that A.A. is distinctly American in keeping with the historic traditions of self-help and pragmatism. The point is well taken, particularly with regard to A.A.'s origins and development. Nevertheless, this has not kept A.A. from taking root in other countries and other cultures as well. In the 1940s, one of my Latin American colleagues expressed doubt that A.A. would ever find acceptance in his culture. The beginnings of A.A. there were slow, it is true. By 1969, there were only 300 Spanish and Portuguese groups in all of Latin America. However, the next 7 years saw an almost 11-fold increase. By 1983, there were over 10,000 groups in Latin America.

Worldwide, in 1982, there were about 20,000 groups in 110 countries other than the U.S. and Canada. This makes a world total of about 50,000 groups with an estimated world total well over a million members.[1]

[1] Henceforth, unless otherwise specified, the group life and organizational references to A.A. will be in terms of the U.S. and Canada. The A.A. groups in

An interesting aspect of this A.A. growth has been a broadening of the composition of its membership.

At first, the members were almost all men. Of the first 100 members, only three were women. As more women appeared, some of the men doubted that the groups could survive an influx of women. Nevertheless, by 1968, when A.A. made its first survey of its membership, women constituted 22% of the total sample. Twelve years later, the 1980 survey showed the proportion of women was up to 31%—and 34% among the members who had come into A.A. during the preceding three years.[2]

Also, the earliest members were so-called low-bottom (late-state) alcoholics. When earlier-stage ("high-bottom") alcoholics began to show up at meetings, many of the old-timers believed that the new people were not "real" alcoholics and hence did not belong to A.A. Today's membership still includes many late-stage alcoholics, but middle-stage and early-stage alcoholics are the majority in most groups.

In A.A.'s early days, there was also skepticism about newcomers as young as 35 or less. Could they possibly be "ready"? Could they have suffered enough? I recall that many professional workers shared this judgment. But by 1980, the survey revealed that the proportion of 35-and-under members to be 26%; and the proportion of those 30-and-under to be almost 15%.

The 1980 survey tells us something else interesting about the members to be found in group meetings, namely, how long they had been sober. (In A.A., this means the time since their last drink.)

---

these two countries have grown up together and continue to be part of a single structure.

[2] The 1980 survey brought responses from 24,950 members in a group sample drawn from every state and province in the U.S. and Canada. The members filled out the survey questionnaire after the meeting at which they had been present. The respondents thus constituted a reasonably representative cross-section of meeting-attending members.

The survey showed that 27% of the members had been sober 5 years or more. It also revealed that 35% of the members had been sober more than one year but less than 5 years. This adds up to 63% of meeting-attenders who had been sober at least a year.

This means, of course, that 37% of the attenders were less than a year from their last drink. This category includes a variety of persons. Many of them had accumulated some months of continuous sobriety since first coming to A.A. Others had experienced an early "slip" (relapse) but were then doing well. We may also assume that others had been slipping periodically but were still trying. Finally, we may assume that a few were still drinking, still trying, or hoping to make a start—or were attending a meeting reluctantly in response to some outside pressure.

But what about the members with 5 years or more of sobriety? How do we account for the survey finding that they constituted only 27% of the meeting-attenders? It is simply the fact that quite a few members, after 3 or 4 years of sobriety, begin to be less active in their groups and begin to attend fewer meetings—or, in some cases, attend practically none at all. Some move out of A.A. altogether. It has been my observation, however, that most sober nonattenders still think of themselves as A.A.'s, continue to associate with some A.A. friends outside of the meeting context, and remain willing to work with an alcoholic whose call for help has come to their particular attention.

We should, of course, keep in mind that groups and meetings vary by the composition of their membership in terms of sobriety length.

We also need to keep in mind that all the talk we hear in A.A. which equates "being sober" with "not drinking" does not mean that not drinking is A.A.'s main criterion for recovery success. Actually, A.A. members also make a distinction between "just being dry" and "sobriety." Sobriety means progress toward good sobriety, and this means a secure and happy sobriety—one which rests on substantial changes in outlook to oneself, to others, and to life.

We turn now to a trend in A.A. which is of particular interest to professional persons. This is the significant change among A.A. members in their attitudes toward professional helpers. Even though there had been significant medical input in the formation of A.A.,[3] and even though the stated A.A. stance toward professionals has always been cooperative, it was not uncommon, in years past, to hear some individual member voicing negative or even disparaging attitudes toward professional helpers who "haven't been there" and therefore "don't understand" and "don't know how to help." Such feelings may indeed have been reinforced by personal experience with one or another professional person. However, such views often had their main root in a member's own prideful or overpossessive feelings about A.A. itself.

Be this as it may, it is important to know that such attitudes are much less prevalent. A substantial change has been occurring and we have documented evidence of the greater openness to professional help.

In A.A.'s 1980 survey, one of the questionnaire clusters referred to "treatment of counseling *other than A.A.*: i.e., medical, psychological, spiritual, etc." which the responding A.A. members had received for their alcoholism *before* coming to A.A.—and *after* being in A.A.

Over half (53%) of the members indicated that they had received such help *before* coming to A.A., and 71% of these indicated that this help "played an important part in directing them to A.A." In short, nearly 38% of the entire sample reported that professional help played not just a role but an important role in their coming to A.A.

---

[3] For the roles of Dr. Wm. Silkworth and "Dr. Bob" the cofounders of A.A., see *Alcoholics Anonymous Comes of Age* (1957) and *Dr. Bob and the Good Oldtimers* (1980).

As for using professional help *after* being in A.A., 40% reported having received such help. Moreover, of this 40%, four out of five (81%) stated that this professional help "played an important part in their recovery from alcoholism." This means that nearly a third (32%) of the entire sample obtained some important, supplementary help from some non-A.A. professional source, after being in A.A.

That this many A.A. members had received professional help in addition to A.A. should revise lingering stereotypes. This survey reinforces my own observation that increasing openness to professional help is definitely a trend among A.A. members. Furthermore, I believe that this trend reflects the improved experiences which A.A. members are having with professional helpers, particularly with professionals in the large number of alcoholism treatment facilities now available.

However, to complete our perspective, we should also note that greater openness to professional help is not evenly distributed throughout A.A. This is illustrated by a small survey I made (Maxwell 1976, p. 440) of treatment experience among A.A. members in the 43 groups in a two-county area. I found that just over 40% of the 1,115 members in these groups had been in a residential treatment center (usually 4 weeks) just before or shortly after coming to A.A. This was the overall trend. But the 43 neighboring groups varied greatly in the proportions of their members who had experienced such a treatment-center exposure. Of the 19 groups with a higher-than-average percentage, 10 groups had proportions of 60% or higher, half of these ranging from 80 to 100%. On the other hand, among the 24 groups with percentages below the average, 14 had proportions below 20%, 6 of them below 10%, including one group in which not a single member had been to a treatment center. These findings show a wide variation in treatment-center experience, even among groups within a small geographic area.

We should add that this is just one illustration of the fact that variability is characteristic of many other aspects of local group life and of individual participation patterns. An adequate perspective on A.A. includes awareness of fellowship-wide patterns or trends on the one hand, and local or individual variations on the other. Otherwise, one can easily be misled by limited contact.

Just as there is a growing openness to professional help among A.A. members, so there appears to be a growing openness to A.A. among professional helpers. This greater interest appears to be reinforced by increasing recognition of the importance of *non*professional contributions to the well-being of people. There seems to be a rediscovery of the potential in *lay* groups.

For one thing, in recent decades, there has been a remarkable proliferation of "self-help" groups—or "mutual-help" groups as I prefer to call them—which have demonstrated their usefulness with a wide range of personal problems: not only alcoholism but also drug addiction, compulsive gambling, mental illness, overeating, bereavement, criminality, etc.—in short, physical, social, and emotional disablements of one kind or another. More and more professional helpers are recognizing the effectiveness of such groups and are learning complementary ways of working with them.[4]

Growing appreciation for lay supportive and therapeutic dynamics is also found in the psychiatric speciality of "community psychiatry." It is obvious that there can never be enough professional help available for the millions and millions of persons who, at some time in their lives, need some degree of help with personal problems. Accordingly, the community psychiatry approach focuses upon the nonprofessional "support" available or potentially available in a community. This

[4] Among those who have been giving thoughtful attention to the self-help or mutual-help movement are Nathan Hurvitz (1974) and Alan Gantner and Frank Riessman (1977) in the United States and David Robinson and Stuart Henry (1977) in England.

includes "natural support systems" of family, neighborhood, and friendship circles; and organized support systems (social organizations and special groups) which are primarily in the hands of nonprofessional persons—or are entirely in the hands of nonprofessionals as in the case of A.A. Gerald Caplan (1974) has explored various ways in which community mental health professionals can relate supportively to these lay support systems without disturbing their lay character and control which he judges to be basic to their effectiveness.

A third development is Yalom's study of group psychotherapy (1975), which provides a theoretical basis for recognizing the therapeutic potential in lay mutual-help groups. In his analysis, he looks behind the differing "fronts" of theory, language, and practice of the various group psychotherapies to identify the shared "core" dynamics which actually produce the constructive, therapeutic changes. Among them, for example, he identifies factors such as acceptance, realizing one is not alone with a particular problem, the instillation of hope, catharsis, interpersonal learning, group cohesion, etc.

In this analysis we have a solid basis for recognizing and understanding many of the dynamics which operate in the social environments not only of professionally directed group psychotherapy but also in the social environments of effective lay mutual-help groups.

Turning to A.A. with these perspectives, we are in a better position to appreciate A.A.'s strengths as a *lay* phenomenon. And it *is* a thoroughly lay operation. It speaks in its own lay language. It looks at alcoholism through the eyes of alcoholics themselves. Furthermore, learning from their own experiences, they have fashioned a lay society with unusual potency.

To be sure, A.A. groups fall short of their own ideal. Often, there is still very immature individual behavior. But what else should we expect when the groups are made up of all kinds of men and women, many not far from their own sick drinking days, and running the full gamut of human shortcomings.

However, it is at this very point that we can observe one of the important therapeutic qualities present in A.A. groups, and this is the remarkable degree of *acceptance*. This does not necessarily mean that everyone likes everyone. Rather, as they listen to each other there is identification with each other. There is acceptance of the other person as a fellow alcoholic—as another imperfect but struggling human being.

On first contact with A.A., a professional person may well question much of what is seen or heard. To become fully cognizant of A.A. dynamics, however, we must go beneath surface appearances.

On the surface, A.A.'s "theory, language, and practice" are different enough to puzzle many professional observers. However, when we look beneath to the core dynamics (as we shall do in later chapters), we find that A.A. has a social environment which is unusually rich with recognized therapeutic factors making for healthy changes in the lives of A.A. members.

Before proceeding, however, it is useful to point out the occasions and settings where the dynamic social and interpersonal interactions take place. A.A. is more than just "meetings."

There are meetings, of course—many meetings. The accessible ones are the "open" meetings which are open to non-A.A. persons as well as members. There are variations in format, but usually they are of the speaker type: generally a leader and two or three speakers who "tell their stories"—how it was with them, what happened, and how it is now. A professional person is welcome at such meetings. Moreover, by attending and also talking informally with a few members afterwards, a professional can learn a great deal about A.A.—and about alcoholics.

More numerous, in most geographic areas, are the "closed" meetings (for alcoholics only) which, typically, are discussion meetings. In these, there is more focus upon specific aspects of the A.A. recovery program and, usually, more free-wheeling and hair-down sharing of personal experience.

Now we come to the significant fact that the greater portion of social interaction in A.A.—and frequently the most potent—does not occur during the actual meetings, but *before* and *after* meetings, and particularly *between* meetings. After the meetings, there is not only the usual lingering and talking right there in the meeting place, but also in the "meeting after the meeting" in a nearby ice cream or coffee shop, in a member's home, or anyplace where some of the group members—in small clusters—will sit around a table and "really talk" for another hour or two.

Still more extensive are the hours of intimate conversations which go on between meeting times when members get together by twos—sometimes more—just about anywhere. It may be in a member's home, office, or any place where two or more can sit down over a cup of coffee. Or, it may be by telephone—day or night. A newcomer is usually given the phone number of one or more members and is encouraged to call. This "telephone therapy" among members is not just for the early weeks or months in A.A., but extends through the years.

Thus, within local groups, there are dyads, triads, and circles of very close relationships. Generally, it is within these intimate clusters that the most uninhibited and meaningful interactions take place, in an atmosphere of caring and mutual trust. If a professional person could, somehow, observe and listen in on all this talk—all this interaction—he or she would have a more intimate and complete view of the very significant dynamics at work. There certainly is much more to the A.A. experience than meets the eye.

However, before we proceed with describing and showing how A.A. experiences mesh with the recovery needs of persons trapped in alcoholism, it is desirable for us to take a very careful look at the nature of alcoholism and its development.

TWO

A World Apart: Becoming Alcoholic

Over the years, as I have talked with professional and other nonalcoholic persons, I have found that a very common difficulty in understanding the A.A. approach has been an insufficient awareness of what the experience of becoming and being alcoholic is like.

This, of course, is not a new problem. As we look back on previous generations, we note that alcoholics have seldom been met with even a minimum of understanding. The problem has generally been perceived in terms of a weak will or moral degeneracy. Occasionally, a "confirmed drunkard" was known to have "reformed"—but not often enough to modify the prevailing judgment: "Just a hopeless drunk."

To be sure, in American history, there have been moments of hope for the "victims of drink." There was the Washingtonian movement of the 1840s which swept the country, and

11

which, during its six or seven years of high activity, rehabilitated somewhere between 100,000 and 150,000 inebriates (Maxwell, 1950; Blumberg, 1977). Again, in the 1870s, there was a substantial revival of successful work with alcoholics by means of the blue-ribbon and red-ribbon "Reform Clubs." While this movement lasted somewhat longer and reached more alcoholics than the Washingtonian movement had, it also failed to leave any permanent change in the attitudes of people or in the institutions of society. Both movements operated in the climate of the temperance movement and did not modify its single-minded devotion to the goal of total abstinence for everybody. Total abstinence just seemed to be more basic: "No alcohol, no drunkards." So it remained through National Prohibition.

In this climate of opinion, the lot of alcoholics was dismal. Society's negative definition of them weighed heavily and usually wore them down. Yet, to some degree, many alcoholics felt, deep down, that the prevailing view of them was somehow incorrect and unjust. They had not set out to become compulsive drinkers. Drinking, at first, had indeed seemed to serve a positive function, enabling them to be themselves more fully, relate better to other people, transcend common human limitations, and feel more in tune with life. They themselves could not understand what had happened to them, neither did they feel that anyone else understood.

Today, we pride ourselves on a better understanding of alcoholics. There is a more accepting attitude toward alcoholic men and women, even though the stigma has by no means disappeared.

In this change, the disease or illness concept of alcoholism has played a key role—serving the important function of moving the problem of alcoholism out of the traditional moral, personal-weakness context into a more contemporary health frame of reference. This is a fundamental and important conceptual shift. Without it, we would have neither A.A. nor the modern alcoholism movement.[1]

But what is the nature of this disease? Why is it that only some drinkers become alcoholic? Here, we run into a wide range of views. Some reflect the traditional perceptions and attitudes. Some views are projections of the moderate- or controlled-drinker's outlook. Even among sophisticated professionals and scientists we find that their interpretations often reflect the limited orientations of specialized disciplines. Consequently, even today, many of the views of nonalcoholics strike alcoholics as still being partial and incomplete. The various views do not seem to do justice to their own inner experience—do not reveal a sufficient acquaintance with the world in which alcoholics live.

Today, of course, there are more professional men and women who *are* able to enter the world of alcoholic persons, at least enough to be helpful. Still others would like to do this, and they will become able to do so as they gain enough experience with alcoholics. However, to date, most professionals and scientists—in fact, most people—have not yet explored this world fully enough for alcoholics to feel that they are really understood.

But, what else should we expect? *In the process of becoming alcoholic, individuals*—no matter what their biological or personality characteristics may have been in their predrinking days—*undergo changes in their perceptions of reality*: changes in their attitudes and values, in their perceptions of themselves and others, and in their feelings about life. Each person's world becomes increasingly different; and, as it does so, it becomes more and more difficult for the average nonalco-

[1] For the classic exposition, see E.M. Jellinek, *The Disease Concept of Alcoholism* (1960). For a more recent review of the concept, see Mark Keller, "The Disease Concept of Alcoholism Revisited," (1976); see also Gitlow (1973) and Vaillant (1983).

holic to comprehend. Increasingly, an alcoholic does come to live in a world apart.

If Alcoholics Anonymous, in certain respects, also appears to be a world apart, a major reason for this lies in the historical fact that A.A. was evolved by alcoholics out of a profound, personal awareness of the world of compulsive drinkers. *In so many ways*, as we shall see, *the two "worlds apart" fit each other*. Consequently, the world of A.A. has some very central features which can be well understood or appraised only to the extent that the inner world of an alcoholic is understood. It takes the latter understanding to appreciate A.A.'s particular ways of coming to grips with an alcoholic's version of reality— and A.A.'s particular ways of facilitating a corrective modification of that distorted view of reality.

Accordingly, before considering the approaches and dynamics of A.A., it is logical and, in fact, indispensable that we take a fresh look at the *process* of becoming alcoholic.

First a clarification. Because the term "alcoholic" is often applied broadly to include more than one kind or pattern of alcoholism, and because there is much confused and futile argument in the alcoholism field simply because the proponents are not talking about the same pattern of alcoholism, it is important for me to make clear what type of alcoholic I am referring to.

The type I am talking about is what Jellinek (1960) called the "gamma" type. Gamma alcoholics are persons whose repetitive increasingly dependent drinking not only produces ill effects upon themselves but is also compulsive to the degree that they are unable consistently to control (1) when they will drink and (2) how much they will drink once started (adapted from Keller and McCormick, 1982).

Gamma alcoholics include a wide variety of individual patterns, as we shall see. However, as a class, gamma alcoholics are distinguished from other types (classes) of alcoholics by the presence of the second inability—the inability consistently to control how much they will drink once started.

The gamma type appears to be the dominant type in the United States and Canada. It is natural, therefore, that the gamma type should have become the model of alcoholism which A.A.'s have in mind when they use the term alcoholic. It helps us to be clear about the type. Accordingly, even though there are other types of alcoholics, it is the gamma type to which I shall be referring in my discussion throughout the book.

For a fresh look at the process of becoming alcoholic, we need not spend time reviewing current etiological research and theorizing.[2] To understand the *experiences* of alcoholic persons, it is more profitable to gain a broad *developmental perspective*.

An adequate developmental perspective requires the recognition that any person's motivation and behavior, at a given time during the process of becoming alcoholic, is the product and function of a very complex, inclusive "field" of forces—dynamic factors—which may be classed as physiological, psychological, cultural, interpersonal, etc.

As Kurt Lewin insisted (1951), those who would explain a person's behavior must allow for *all* possible variables which affect behavior. Lewin's field concept serves as a constant reminder that any single factor is but one of myriad factors which are in dynamic relationship to each other.

Furthermore, an adequate developmental perspective includes the recognition that a change in one area of a given person's field of motivating forces brings about modifications throughout the entire field. It also includes the recognition that a given person's field keeps changing throughout life. We

[2] The reader, interested in contemporary perspectives on the etiology of alcoholism, may find one or more of these recent publications useful: Bacon (1973), Gomberg (1982), Goodwin (1982), Royce (1981), Vaillant (1983), Wallace (1972), White (1982), and Zinberg (1981).

should note that a field perspective does not in any way discount the effects of early life experiences. However, it does give realistic weight to all later circumstances, experiences, and responses.

Not only does a person's field keep changing, but, in the case of future alcoholics (and here we come to the heart of the matter), *the drinking itself begins to change the field.* Over time, there is an increasing change in the *meaning* and *use* of alcohol as the physical, behavioral, and social effects of increased drinking feed back upon the body, mind, and emotions of the drinker.

Early on or later, future alcoholics give drinking what Bales (1946) called a "utilitarian" meaning. That is, their *use* of alcohol is not primarily for ritual, dietary, or strictly social or customary reasons, but to feel better, to counter stress, ease anxiety, smooth existence, alter consciousness—to feel and be able to act more like the person the drinker would like to be.

Quickly or gradually, the drinking experiences of future alcoholics are such that they come to give more than a mild utilitarian meaning to drinking. Whatever the physiological and psychological factors which may be involved in a given case, a special and strong utilitarian bond is formed—a positive mental and emotional association or relationship with drinking. As more than one alcoholic has put it: "I fell in love with it." To the degree that this occurs, a new and significant factor enters the picture—comes to operate in that person's motivational field. The rewards of more drinking reinforce the utilitarian meaning and attractiveness of drinking. This occurs over and over, and in this repetitive process, what I call the "drinking relationship" grows in strength and importance until it becomes a central force in the drinker's life.[3]

[3] The utility and appropriateness of the term "relationship" in this context was first suggested to me in lectures by Vernon Johnson. See his book, *I'll Quit Tomorrow* (1980).

To initiate this special relationship, drinking must be experienced as particularly rewarding—more rewarding than merely relaxing a little, or adding a little something extra to the celebration of a meaningful event, or enjoying a party a little more. Some alcoholics report a very striking initial reward, sometimes with their very first drinking experience. Conversely, there are those for whom the rewards appear to have been relatively mild at first but increased substantially in the course of some years of social drinking. But quickly or slowly, in feeling and thinking, the future alcoholic develops a *special*, *personal*, *powerful*, and *enduring* relationship with drinking— a relationship which *eventually becomes compulsive*. Not fully appreciating the power and enduring quality of this acquired relationship is probably the greatest lack in many professionals' understanding of alcoholism.

The initial meaningful reward may be just the "trip," getting "high," becoming intoxicated, experiencing a transcendent unity of being. This is illustrated in the following statements by A.A. members:

I had been a teetotaler in my youth, and life was fun. But that first drink of wine gave me such a high that from there on I wanted more of it. (Female)

I was a kid of 16, and I loved that first drink. I got drunk, but I loved it. And the next time, I got drunk again and still loved it. (Male)

I was introduced to booze in the form of wine at the age of 14 and I fell in love with it. For 25 years after that, I tried to find the same warm glow that that first drink gave me. (Male)

Frequently, in addition to the pleasure of tripping, there are substantial *social* rewards—belongingness in a group, convivial enjoyment of others. There are many drinking groups in which regular drinking with frequent drunkenness is the accepted and approved social activity.

More often, however, the reported initial reward is a greater sense of competency or comfort in a social setting: "I could dance." "I could say what I wanted to say." "It made me feel more at ease with people." "It made me feel free with people."

My first drinking was deliberate, for the purpose of overcoming timidity with girls at dances and parties. (Male)

When I discovered that alcohol could take away my shyness in a social situation, I said, "Aha! This is it!" From there on there was no socializing without alcohol. (Female)

My inferiority feelings and my tendencies to introversion rather isolated me from people. Alcohol broke down my inhibitions, and I felt perfectly at home in any situation. (Male)

In addition to pleasure, the common denominator in the above initial rewards is the *experiencing of oneself as being more acceptable in some respect*. It may be in terms of some particular area of one's functioning, or it may be an improved general sense of self:

As a kid I had a happy family life. But there was always an inner yearning to discover new heights which I eagerly tried. I traveled all over the country and was on the go constantly. Not only did I discover new heights, I also discovered alcohol, and to my amazement, A NEW ME. . . . I immediately fell in love with drinking. (Male)

I was outwardly very successful and felt very self-sufficient. But, there was still a vague unrest that bothered me. Then, I learned that a martini would dissolve this basic inner feeling. It would make me feel better put together. (Female)

Having discovered the "magic of a drink," the drinker has learned that he or she now has a tool for making the experience of life more satisfactory. It is a tool which *works*. Moreover, the person learns that it will work whenever it is employed—

that it is dependable. And it acts quickly. Such immediately rewarded (reinforced) behavior is likely to be repeated—even more likely to be repeated if the felt reward is substantial.

With this new tool and the freedom it gives, the future alcoholic typically enters a period of years of what he or she looks upon as "happy drinking." Life is much more the way it ought to be. Indeed, for a time, the drinking may not appear to be different from the social drinking of many who never become alcoholics. But, to a greater or lesser degree, there is a difference in the *personal meaning* given to drinking—a difference in the *relationship* to drinking. And, *if* the drinking continues to be sufficiently rewarding, and *if* the total field permits or encourages more drinking (e.g., being in fairly heavy drinking circles), the difference in personal meaning grows. The drinking becomes a more important and a more frequently used tool.

In fact, the most significant development during this period of "successful drinking" (in the case of a future alcoholic, to repeat) is the *increasing value and use given to alcohol—drinking more often, on more occasions, for more purposes*, and *drinking more at a time*. Even though the drinking is still felt to be "good," the drinking itself is changing the drinker's field in ways which increase both the importance and the use of alcohol. There is a *growing anticipation* of drinking times—a *growing preoccupation* with drinking. Emotionally and physically, drinking is becoming *more essential*. All this usually occurs before obvious negative or undesirable consequences are experienced.

Accordingly, all factors which contribute to the increased use and importance of alcohol during this still nonproblem period belong in our developmental perspective.

One such important factor, according to Cahalan's findings (1970), is "environmental support of heavy drinking." Such heavy-drinking social circles are common in our society and contribute significantly to the increased use and importance of drinking for many future alcoholics.

During this problem-free period, an increase in the importance and use of alcohol is also fostered by what has been called the *pampering* effect of repeated drinking. Because drinking works not only well and quickly but also effortlessly, its use is easily extended to other times, situations, and purposes for which it was not needed or used before. More and more, previously satisfying activities give way to simple elbow bending.

If we take all these factors into account—a heavy-drinking social environment, the pampering effect, and add whatever physiological vulnerabilities there may be in a given case—we can more readily understand how even psychologically "normal" persons can proceed into heavier and heavier drinking. A mildly utilitarian definition of drinking can gradually be modified in favor of more and more use of alcohol—and changed into an increasingly potent relationship with drinking.

But, in addition to all the factors leading to heavier drinking, the *heavier drinking itself* has significant physiological consequences. Bodily adaptation to the heavier intake manifests itself in increased tolerance and some degree of physiological *dependence*. In the overall process of becoming alcoholic, increased tolerance and growing dependence are significant changes—objective warning signs. However, the alcohol which has been working so well up to this point can also be used to take care of such undesired physiological changes. Accordingly, drinking is stepped-up as needed. And, because the physiological changes do not show themselves with dramatic suddenness, the accommodation to them may scarcely be noticed. There may, at times, be a vague recognition of drinking more, but at this stage, future alcoholics are most likely still to think of themselves as normal, social drinkers. It is self-deception, but it keeps them going.

No matter when, early or late, or in what order such changes come (and the patterns do vary), these are the kinds of development which usually occur during the years (sometimes, many years) of essentially problem-free drinking.[4]

Drinking becomes an even more potent field modifier when the meaning and use of alcohol are extended to deal with the *more distressing negative consequences* of heavier and heavier drinking. One such common extension—and an important one—was well described by an A.A. speaker at an open meeting.

Jim had his first drink when he was a senior in college. His first job put him into drinking circles in a major city. He said that he liked what drinking did for him and began drinking quite a bit like the other "happy, normal drinkers" around him. Overseas, in World War II, his drinking increased— eventually increased enough to interfere with his former level of performance. But, with extra effort, he was still achieving. However, after returning to civilian life, the physiological effects of his heavy drinking finally became such that he felt forced into morning drinking, something he had abhorred before. As Jim tells it:

Things came to the point where if I had the normal fruit juice or coffee in the morning, I spent the next five minutes with my head in the hopper. Nothing would stay down. Oh, the sweat and the promises: "Dear God, get me out of this, and I'll never do it

---

[4] Some alcoholics, looking back, believe that they never really were social drinkers—that they had drunk "alcoholically" from the start. They say that, from the first, alcohol had meant more to them than to others: "I always drank more than I intended;" or "I got drunk when the others didn't;" or "I always drank to get drunk." But, even for most (not all) of these persons, problems from drinking were not significant at first but, rather, developed in the course of heavy drinking. Such persons may have had a running start, but what they report is not yet alcoholism as I am using the term. It takes time to become an alcoholic—a short time, in some cases, but time.

again." So I learned to take the morning drink. It stopped the shakes. I could shave. Another healthy belt and I felt pretty good, and I would get dressed. Then maybe another healthy belt and even a cup of coffee would stay down.

What is important about this kind of development? Like Jim, heavy drinkers, at this point, learn a very meaningful new fact about alcohol which extends its use significantly. They learn that even the distressing, physical consequences of excessive drinking such as hangovers, tremors, and nausea can be overcome by some more drinking and that they can then *again be in control*. All along, they had been reinforcing their learning that drinking "works" and works particularly well. And, now that drinking has produced unwanted and painful consequences, there comes the greatly reassuring discovery that alcohol will work even here. Sure, most of them probably knew this fact intellectually, having heard it from others. But, now, they know "in gut fact" that drinking can handle crises such as these—in addition to serving all the prior purposes for which it had been used. In this demonstration, the already strong drinking relationship is reinforced substantially.

Of course, this extended use of drinking also increases their physical and psychological dependency upon alcohol. Drinking takes on an even greater urgency. This is commonly manifested by gulping the first drink or two for a speedier effect. Because of the increased tolerance, the drinkers "need" more alcohol than is customary even in their fairly heavy drinking circles. Because they do not want others to notice, they become clever at sneaking extra drinks at a party, or if the chances of doing so are slim, they "prime the pump" with a few extra drinks before going to the party to make absolutely certain that they will have enough.

The eventual strength and centrality of the relationship to alcohol is well illustrated in another A.A. member's story.

This man had taken a trip with his son to attend a ceremonial event. He made sure that he would have plenty of gin and vermouth with him. They checked in at a motel and went to the ceremony. Upon returning to the motel, they found that their room had been ransacked. Gone were the clothes, luggage, shaving gear—also the gin and vermouth. He described what happened: "I raced to the manager's desk, and there I raised all sorts of Cain because my gin and vermouth were missing. After a bit, my son, standing there, said, 'Tell him about our luggage and clothes.' Well, you know, it's the absolute truth: it simply didn't occur to me that our good bags were gone—the clothes and everything else."

The consequences of heavy drinking which we have been discussing, up to this point, can be taken care of by more drinking. But there are other consequences which *cannot* be offset by drinking. And, these seriously compound the drinker's problems by decreasing his ability to function in a satisfactory or socially expected manner.

Blackouts (memory lapses) are among such very common dysfunctional developments. Not being able to remember one's activity during a period of time the day or evening before can be embarrassing to say the least—if, for example, the activity was a business transaction. In any case, and for a variety of reasons, repeated blackouts are a most unwanted and worrisome development. They increase the anxiety level and also distort the drinker's perception of his own behavior and the reactions of others to it.

However, the most critical consequence of the years of excessive drinking is the onset of the inability to drink according to intention—intending to have only a few drinks but getting drunk anyway.

At first, this new type of control loss may happen only once or twice in, say, ten drinking episodes and will likely be rationalized away: something eaten that evening, the extra pressure at work that day, the quarrel that day with boss or spouse, etc. But when it happens more often, particularly on occasions when it is very inappropriate and when there was determination to stay within proper bounds, this new development becomes very disturbing. There has been negative feedback before from some of the people around, but this kind of uncontrolled behavior is completely out of order and brings strong negative reactions from others.

Moreover, this kind of behavior is not up to the drinker's own expectations. It is unacceptable, and it is bewildering. Can it be (perish the thought) that alcohol, the trusted friend, can no longer be counted on? A great feature about drinking all these years has been its dependability in enhancing self-esteem and feelings about life. Drinking has even brought under control certain negative consequences of heavy drinking. It has been very reliable—and extremely important. For it to become undependable presents a fearsome prospect.

How is this serious development met? Usually, by simply attempting to make it *untrue*. This loss of control is too devastating a fact to accept, so alcoholics attempt to deny it by a two-pronged tactic: (1) by trying through *strenuous efforts at controlled drinking* to prove that control has not been lost; and (2) by *rationalizing* and *projecting*—finding other explanations, including placing the blame elsewhere.

However, their struggle to control their drinking does not really work. Things get worse. Their anxieties about their dilemma increase. Rationalizations are added to rationalizations as they depart more and more from customary and acceptable drinking behavior, and become less and less able to live up to the general expectations of others—or of themselves. Their increasing deviations bring not only negative social reactions but also progressively isolate them from customary and satisfying relationships with the persons around them. Their views of reality, of themselves, of other people, and of life become more and more distorted. They come to feel more and more cut off from people—and more and more cut off from life. It is a vicious downward spiral, for the more cut off they feel, the more they feel impelled to use alcohol to regain at least temporary emotional contact with people and life—or, at times, to anesthetize the increasingly intolerable pain of existence.

However, it becomes more and more of a losing game. Their bodies take an increased beating. The emotional constrictions and the painful anxieties increase—at an accelerating rate. Fear of withdrawal pains may become a stronger motivation for drinking than any previous anticipation of reward. More and more, they move to the point where they are drinking to live—and living to drink. As one who had reached this point put it: "My world had become the next drink."

Such is the basic story of those who become what A.A. members call "low-bottom" alcoholics—definitely late-stage alcoholics.

As was noted earlier, the first A.A. members were all low-bottom alcoholics. They were skeptical about newcomers who showed less physical, psychological, social, or economic damage, wondering if they could really be alcoholics.

Nevertheless, the low- and high-bottom alcoholics soon found common ground. True, the drinking of the high-bottom newcomers had not taken them down as far. However, as they listened to each other, it was apparent to them that their respective roads, despite individual variations, were essentially alike. The drinking of the high-bottom alcoholics had also reached a point of sufficient centrality in their lives so that unacceptable problems had developed. Furthermore, the need to drink had become a force powerful enough so that their own efforts to control or stop their drinking had proven to be ineffectual.

To put some flesh and blood into the process of becoming an alcoholic, let us turn in the next chapter to the personal experiences of a variety of A.A. members—men and women who describe, in their own words, what becoming an alcoholic was like.

THREE
What We Were Like

In the previous chapter, I focused on the *process* of becoming alcoholic—the process of learning to use alcohol as a personal aid in the everyday business of living—and the process of *coming to rely upon it more and more* in order to feel and act more like the person one would like to be, to enhance living, to feel more alive. It is a process in the course of which a deeply meaningful *relationship* with drinking grows and becomes more and more powerful.

I have also viewed the inception and development of this potent relationship in terms of the drinker's total field of motivational factors—a field which is made up of physiological, psychological, cultural, and interpersonal variables—*all of them*! Furthermore, all the variables are understood to be interrelated so that any change in one part of the field brings about changes throughout the entire field.

But how do these changes appear to the individual alcoholic? From the inside, in experiential terms, what are the changes in thinking, feeling and perception which occur? How does the alcoholic's changing world look and feel?

Such a fleshing-out of the field-change process will be useful to us professionally by deepening our understanding of the alcoholics we see—and by increasing our capacity to relate to them. Such an inside view can also make us more aware of the nature and broad range of personal changes which "recovery" logically includes.

Such an inside look is particularly important in this book because it will serve to sensitize us to the ways in which A.A. works—the ways in which the A.A. program and social environment help to bring about the field changes which spell recovery.

I shall be drawing upon the experiences of a variety of A.A. members, men and women, as described, for the most part, in taped interviews. Some quotes are from stories told in A.A. meetings. Unless references are given, this is all unpublished material.

To manage the almost infinite number of variables involved in the process of becoming alcoholic, I will focus attention upon the *changes in attitude and behavior* with regard to four key areas: (1) the drinking itself, (2) the self, (3) other persons, and (4) one's outlook on life.

First, the drinking. The following two excerpts describe the major changes with regard to the *use of alcohol*:

The line between social and alcoholic drinking is difficult for me to draw. If social drinking is when it does not cause you trouble, then I drank socially probably up to age 30. Then, I began having a little trouble. However, I don't believe I had a real compulsion to drink for another 3 years. But, then there were about 9 years of real, out-of-control, alcoholic drinking before I came to A.A. (at age 42). It was a *slow and insidious process—until the very end, when this process speeded up.* (54-M-12/0)[1]

I would say I had about 12 years of drinking of which the last 5 years were alcoholic drinking. The first 7 years were the enjoyable-type drinking. The last 5 years were getting pretty rough. The last 2 or 3 years were real troublesome—I was getting into a lot of trouble with the law, and the family, and work. It got so bad I had to do something about it. (41-M-5/10)

The next three accounts illustrate a *variety* of drinking patterns and attitudes toward drinking, and particularly *the differing lengths of time before drinking got out of control*:

I began drinking when I was about 40. Because of my Baptist background, I really felt that it was a big sin. I really did. That bugged me the most. I thought I drank in rebellion against my husband. *How fast the drinking overtook me* is another thing which frightened me. I had thought that people who were alcoholics had been drunks all their lives. I really got snow-balled in a hurry. Finally, after many months of heavy drinking every night and not being able to stop, I went to a counselor. . . . I just had the feeling that drinking was taking over and I didn't like that. (52-F-0/4)

Another woman with a quite different drinking career:

I drank for 40 years (from age 22 to 62)—*always drank a lot. Most of my companions drank.* I was married twice and *both of my husbands drank as heavily as I did.* My work wasn't really affected by my drinking until the last stages—about the last 7 years. Things came to a head with a 3-day drunk. I don't remember what happened to me over those 3 days. The only thing I can recall was coming to, looking around my apartment,

---

[1] This code refers to the respondent's age at the time of interview, sex, and years/months since the last drink. All emphases in this and other responses are added by the author.

and saying to myself: "I need help!"—and then calling A.A. (65-F-2/11)

A high-bottom man:

I had 23 years of social drinking and about 1½ years of alcoholic drinking. I was generally an evening drinker. A good many times it was business-lunch drinking. But toward the end, it was morning, noon, and night drinking. My life had become unmanageable in that the drinking affected the soundness of my business decisions. My family life was very, very rocky—no communications, and the kids were upset. (44-M-0/6)

In the following, we have an example of a man whose alcoholism did not develop until he was in *retirement*. True, he retired early, but this also occurs among persons who retire at 65 or even later:

I began my social drinking in college when I was 21 and continued social drinking until I retired from the Army at 50. I believe my alcoholic drinking started about 4 years later—and lasted about 4 years before I went for treatment.

I drank bourbon and water for most of my social drinking and for perhaps 2 years of my alcoholic drinking. Then, I switched to vodka—vodka and tonic or just straight vodka out of the bottle. I drank only in the evening at first, starting before dinner with three or four highballs. This graduated into drinking at lunch, and this went on for a year or so. Then it got so that I required drinking in the morning, and this graduated into drinking around the clock for about the last 4 months.

Just prior to going to a treatment center, my alcoholism had affected my work, my family life, and my social life. *I reached the point where I thought that I didn't have a friend in the world—and couldn't care less. I lived only for alcohol.* (59-M-1/10)

This man had not been "living only for alcohol" earlier in his drinking career. Nevertheless, I assume that at least *some degree* of the special relationship to drinking was present before retirement. During those years, the total field, including job responsibilities, operated to keep drinking from getting out of hand. Once the field was substantially changed by retirement, the existing relationship to alcohol was allowed to grow and gain a more central place.

Whether it comes late or early, slowly or quickly, after a person's drinking definitely begins to get out of control and the person becomes intoxicated when he or she doesn't want to, *controlled drinking* gets to be the name of the game. Giving up drinking altogether is by now unthinkable, so controlled drinking is seen as the only tolerable compromise—the only hope of avoiding more trouble. As one member quipped: "The problem was how to drink and stay sober."

The effort at control becomes an increasingly strenuous struggle: will power pitted against a growing compulsion. All kinds of "logical" strategies to limit drinking are devised—changing the times of drinking or the places of drinking or the types of drink. One man purchased a set of green glasses for his drinks, thinking the color would somehow increase his ability to resist drinking so much.

One of the most common strategies tried is *going on the wagon*. The strength of the relationship, however, is such that there is seldom any intention of doing so permanently. The main purpose usually is to get others off one's back—to *prove* to others and to oneself that loss of control does not really exist, and/or to demonstrate that the drinker *does* have will power and *can* manage the problem *all alone*. This, and eventual disillusionment with the effort, is well illustrated in the following accounts:

Approximately a year prior to A.A., I lost a job as a result of my drinking. My productivity had gone to zero. And just prior to A.A., my family was about to break up. I had also begun some binge drinking where I would lose 2 or 3 days at a time. Then, I went on a period of self-imposed sobriety and stayed without a drink for about 3 months. *I knew I was going to drink again, but I was sort of proving to myself that I wasn't an alcoholic and that I could control it.* Then, when I started to drink again, within a couple of weeks I was right back to where I had been before. Before long, I woke up after a lost weekend, about 2 or 3 o'clock on Monday morning, in a complete state of panic. I just had to talk to somebody. So I called A.A. because I had heard that they answered the phone 24 hours a day. (38-M-3/2)

I probably had 27 years of social drinking and possibly 6 years of alcoholic drinking. I was a periodic drinker. My family relationships became very strained because of my drinking, and I wanted "off the merry-go-round." After succeeding in being dry for 15 months or so, I drank again. That drunk was a "one-bottle drunk" but it brought me to my knees and I knew that I needed help. (48-F-1/11)

About 3 years ago, I went 7 months without drinking. I thought I was doing great, and I let everyone know about it. But, then I picked up a drink . . . and found out that I just couldn't handle my problem on my own. So I went to a treatment center where I was introduced to A.A. (39-M-0/9)

Usually, the failure of the effort to control the drinking is very difficult to acknowledge. As previously indicated, alcohol is by now so important that the reality of loss of control—and all that it implies—simply has to be rationalized away. Rationalizations probably have been employed before to deal with some of the undesired efforts of excessive drinking. With loss of control, the need becomes even greater. Rationalizations are added to rationalizations until we have an "alibi structure" which is often built up to a point of unbelievable *denial*.[2] Consider the following account:

The areas of my life most affected by my drinking were my family and my job. Things were getting increasingly worse at home. My children feared me. My mood changes were obvious.

[2] A very perceptive and thorough discussion of the dynamics of denial is offered by Margaret Bean (1981).

One moment I'd be calm, and the next I would be screaming mad. They didn't know what to expect of me. And my wife was very unhappy with my drinking also. And my boss was getting increasingly upset with my behavior. In fact, the day before going into an alcoholism treatment center, I had reported to work after drinking several martinis. I left work, drank more martinis and reported back again in a drunken condition. Mind you, I was in a mangement position with the corporation, and I returned to work drunk in front of all the other employees.

That's why I went to the treatment center the next day. But note, I didn't go for my alcoholism. *My sole purpose was to get a letter from the treatment center stating that I was NOT an alcoholic*, so that I could continue with my drinking. (38-M-0/6)

This is a striking illustration of how much an alcoholic's view of reality can become distorted—also, of how tactics are shaped by that distorted perception. This man saw that he *had* to do something to hold his job. This much was realistic. But the only problem with drinking that he was able to perceive, at the time, was the need to obtain some sort of official green light to continue drinking. A story like this told in an A.A. meeting will produce gales of laughter. The members can identify with the speaker. They remember their own denials— and some of the ludicrous things they themselves had done— all so logical at the time.

An almost classic description of the struggle to control the drinking, and the final disillusionment with that self-effort, is found in the following:

Until I was about 32, I did heavy weekend drinking. But then it started to occur during the week, once or twice; and in the final stages, it was 5 out of 7 days. Just prior to coming into the program, my marriage had terminated because of alcohol. I had gotten into a serious auto accident which cost me a job. Before that, I had had a series of jobs and was quite dissatisfied with them because of my drinking.

For some years, I had tried to control my drinking. I promised myself that *I could do it alone*—that *I could stop drinking*—or *I could limit my drinking*—or *I could forsee my probable actions*. When I lost grasp of all these things, when *I couldn't stop drinking*, and when *I couldn't predict the day that I was gonna drink*, and when the *events that happened while I was drinking were completely out of my control*—that is, when my life had become unmanageable and depressed, that's when I joined A.A. (41-M-1/2)

However, even when there is a realization of loss of control, a common way of dealing with the dilemma of obsessively wanting to keep on drinking despite unwanted consequences is to *postpone doing anything about it*. Often, it takes a *crisis* of some kind to sharpen the realization to the point of action:

The last 2 or 3 years of my drinking were real troublesome. I was getting into a lot of trouble with the law, and the family, and work. I realized for a long time that I had a drinking problem but like most alcoholics I *procrastinated* in doing anything about it. But, when I finally got into trouble with the law—a bad accident through drinking—*and it seeemed like the world was caving in on me* and I had nowhere else to turn, I came to A.A. to find out why certain things happened to me that didn't happen to other people who I thought drank as much as I did. (41-M-5/10)

This man did not yet know what he would have to do about his problem, but he did get off dead-center.

The *strength* of the relationship to alcohol is underscored by every example of the strenuous struggle to bring an evermore out-of-control situation under control. And it would seem that the very struggle to control the drinking actually increases the compulsiveness of the "need" to drink—makes the relationship to alcohol still more powerful and central.

One man's recognition of the relationship's strength is poignantly depicted in the following:

After about 20 years of social drinking and 8 years of alcoholic drinking, every department of my life was affected. My drinking was out of control. I *knew* that I was going to lose my wife and family. I *knew* that I was going to lose my job. I was what you might call a "medium high-bottom drunk;" I had money in the bank. I had a job and everything else, but I *knew* that within 6 months or so I was going to lose it all. My last vivid impression, before I came into the program, was seeing a beggar on the street begging money for a glass of beer and wondering how long it would be before I would be in that same condition. (70-M-15/7)

The nature and strength of an alcoholic's relationship with alcohol are also brought out by the statements which alcoholics used to describe their relationship. They are worth noting:

I took to alcohol.
I fell in love with alcohol.
I discovered the joy of booze.
How can you have a good time without alcohol?
It was my wonder drug.
Alcohol became my friend—and eventually, my only friend.
I accepted drinking in its entirety.
My mind was computerized (programmed) to live with booze.
I loved liquor more than I loved anything or anyone.
I lived only for alcohol.
Alcohol was my god.

The statements above not only describe the special relationship to alcohol, but also underscore the eventual *centrality* and *obsessive strength* of the relationship.

Viewing the greatly intensified relationship with drinking as the key change in becoming alcoholic does not minimize the seriousness of the *interrelated* field changes—the changes in the alcoholic's self-perception, changes in relationships with other persons, and changes in feelings about life in general.

The changes in thinking and feeling about one's *self* come through loud and clear in the following accounts:

I never dreamed that something I immediately fell in love with—my wonder drug—would also be the same thing that would lead to the almost total collapse of my self-being. (Male)

I probably had 10 years of alcoholic drinking. As a social drinker, I began as a very fussy drinker. If people were not scotch drinkers and didn't go to the best places, I'd have no part of them. But, *as alcohol became more and more important to me*—and AS ALCOHOL TOOK ME AWAY FROM MYSELF, I lowered my standards and ultimately I would accept anything that anybody offered because *I had to have it to exist*. (63-F-23/1)

My own self-image just really went to hell over a 2-year period before I got into A.A. I was at a complete loss. I was thinking that I *might just disappear* or something—*become a non-entity*—if something didn't happen with the drinking. (38-M-0/3)

I had the feeling that I was *losing myself*. (40-F-0/3)

I didn't have any of the horrible experiences that so many alcoholics have had. . . . I slept in a bed and I slept in pajamas, and I did bathe. *But, I wasn't anything inside—simply nothing!* (Male)

At the end, I became *a zero—a nothing*! (Female)

Such changes in self-image or self-perception do not occur unrelated to equally great changes in one's perceptions of, and relationships to, *others*.

I started drinking when I was 15. I always drank with the idea that I wanted to get drunk. I was a periodic drinker in the beginning, and then it increased. Every single area of my life was being affected by my alcoholism. My *business* (at that time I was in my own business) and my *marital life* had been affected. *My children had been taken away from me* because of my drinking. *All the people that were near to me had turned away from me and I felt totally alone.* I was 38 years old, *totally addicted* and TOTALLY ALONE. (42-F-3/9)

Nor do the great changes in self-perception and in relations to others occur without great changes in one's general outlook on life. These dimensions are all interrelated and are brought out in the following:

I had *completely lost all of the good feelings I had about myself.* My thinking was very irrational. There was a *complete change of personality*, inside especially. I went from an extrovert to an introvert. I cut myself off, very much, from everybody. I was *isolated, lonely, and spiritually almost dead.* (43-M-1/4)

Of course, to varying degrees, the functioning of the body is affected as well—along with all the other changes in perception of oneself, others, and the world:

My drinking had affected me in all categories—*physical condition—not able to work*—had the *shakes. Resentments* of things that happened in my past. *Self-pity. Spiritually, not believing in anything*—MAD AT THE WHOLE WORLD! (55-M-14/10)

In the following accounts, we have thumbnail descriptions of both the drinking progression and the overall state of mind and affairs before finally deciding to seek help:

I drank daily. At the beginning, I would get drunk about once every 6 weeks. Toward the end, I was getting drunk just about 6 times a week. I'd say prior to A.A., my family life was affected, my financial security was drastically affected, and my wife was about ready to leave. I had lost my job. *Spiritually, I was bankrupt—nothing*! It affected everything. *I thought I was just going insane.* (28-M-0/5)

I had about 10 years of social drinking and 4 years of alcoholic drinking. In the beginning, drinking made me feel like a life-of-the-party type of person. But the last couple of years were very depressing and full of despair. I was drinking almost daily. I would try to stop—and mean it when I said it—but once I picked up the first drink, I couldn't stop. Even when I asked for help, I didn't fully realize that all areas of my life were affected: my whole home, my children, my working habits. I couldn't function. I realize now that *I was broken down physically, mentally*, and *spiritually*. I HAD LOST MY WHOLE DRIVE FOR LIVING. (40-F-6/11)

I had about 20 years of social drinking and 10 of alcoholic drinking. *My life was completely shot.* My family life was at a standstill. My social life was nil. I spent as much of the 24 hours of the day as I could in bed with a bottle. I couldn't see how a program for living like A.A. could help me where everything else had failed. But, I had reached bottom and was willing to give anything a try. (50-F-1/4)

The later phases of the process of becoming alcoholic might be summed up in simple, common-denominator terms:

"My drinking eventually began to take me away from myself, away from other people and away from life. This, in turn, led me to depend more and more on alcohol to give me back to myself, back to others and to life—even if only for a little while. But things only got worse. My drinking got more and more out of control, and increasingly I was losing control of my life. My self-esteem went down and down—and I felt more and more cut off from people—and more and more cut off from life. I could neither control the drinking which had brought me to this state, nor could I leave it alone. But, at the time, it was very hard to accept the reality of all this—that this had really happened to *me*. Extremely difficult! What's more, it was impossible to picture a satisfactory life without alcohol."

How does A.A. meet such an alcoholic person "where he is at"? How does A.A. help such a person to restructure his world—his total field? In particular, how does A.A. help the person to achieve a new stance with regard to drinking, a new view of other persons, of life, and at the same time, of himself?

We can interpret many A.A. dynamics in terms of almost any school of psychotherapy. Much of my own thinking has been in these terms. However, I have gradually come to the view that A.A. is more readily and completely understood if we also look upon it as a new society—a tailor-made and very potent new social and cultural environment in which the requisite new learning takes place.

In the next chapter, the focus will be on the beginnings of involvement in the new society

FOUR
Entering a New Society

The last two chapters have outlined and illustrated the intertwining elements of the process by which drinking moves to center stage in the life of an alcoholic person. I have viewed the total development as both the product of, and the producer of, physiological, psychological, and social changes throughout the person's total field—changes which reach the point where the person becomes unable, by himself, to keep his drinking under nondamaging control—or to leave it alone.

Also presented were personal accounts of the field changes which had occurred—in particular, the development of a special and eventually compulsive relationship to alcohol, a great reduction in self-esteem, and an increasing estrangement from other persons—and from life.

As stated earlier, it is difficult for a nonalcoholic to grasp the extent of the changes—or to explain them. I have touched on the defensive and reassurance functions of *rationalization* and *projection* in making the alcoholic person's behavior more acceptable to himself. But, the cost of these mechanisms is a gross distortion of the person's perception of reality. The same is true of *repression*, the unconscious banishment from consciousness of unacceptable thoughts and feelings. These defenses are all means by which the person tries to manage increased anxiety, guilt, and even periodic remorse. How effective they can be in distorting reality is strikingly illustrated in the following account:

> I had reached the stage where I couldn't cope without alcohol, and I couldn't cope with alcohol. My life had become one total mess. I cried in the morning, in the afternoon, and at night. I couldn't remember what day it was. I couldn't remember when I had done something, like talking to somebody—whether it was this afternoon, this morning, or a week ago. I had trouble eating. I thought about suicide, but I didn't have the nerve. I had come to the point where the only answer seemed to be for me to leave—walk out—and never come back.
>
> But I didn't think I was an alcoholic. I was convinced that circumstances made it necessary for me to drink. If those circumstances would be cleared up, I felt that my drinking would stop and that I could become a good mother and a normal person again. It was circumstances. I really believed that until I came into A.A. (33-F-0/8)

Perception of reality is also distorted by the memory *blackouts* which most alcoholics experience with increasing frequency.

Heavy drinking also intensifies the normal mental processes of *selective attention* and of *selective recall*. The drinker remembers the party of the evening before, but some of his own actions, or the reactions of other persons around him, cannot be recalled because they were not really registered in the first place. Of those that are registered, it is the pleasant impressions that are recalled, and even exaggerated, and the person is absolutely disbelieving when told what he had really said or done. "It just couldn't have been like that!"

When we give full weight to the reality-distorting dynamics, we can comprehend the alcoholic's increasing inability to see what he or she is really doing, to perceive the severity of the problem. We can also appreciate how *fears* intensify the distorting processes—particularly the fear of a life without alcohol. The more central the role of alcohol has become in the alcoholic's life, the more difficult it is to imagine living in any satisfactory way without alcohol. As one member put it in A.A.'s monthly magazine:

> During the drinking years, the alcoholic tends to relate more and more of his life to liquor and to make it the hub of his activities and even his thinking—gradually at first and then rapidly.
>
> Then, when he has come to the realization that he can no longer control his drinking and that, in fact, he cannot by himself even stop it, he has great difficulty visualizing anything but a dreary life without liquor. Since the drinking has become an integral part of his life, he cannot see how much will be left if that is removed.[1]

Alcoholics coming into A.A., of course, show varying degrees and patterns of reality distortion. But there *is* distortion. And this distorted version is the reality of an alcoholic's "world apart." It is a reality in which an alcoholic has a firm belief because his or her own experiences, as perceived, have confirmed it over and over. To the would-be helper it seems like a walled-in world, impervious to the facts and views of the generally accepted reality of the surrounding society.

Even when an alcoholic's confidence in the validity of his

[1] *A.A. Grapevine*, September, 1948. Reprinted by permission.

own reality had been shaken enough to go to A.A. or to seek out professional help of some kind, he is still anchored in his alcoholic world, unable to get a clear fix on his total situation.

Another barrier to be overcome is his strenuous resistance to defining his problem as alcoholism. It is not just the social stigma. It is more. To admit loss of control over drinking is like admitting *personal* defeat—being at least some kind of failure in life.

Usually, alcoholic persons also have various *misconceptions about A.A.* Many will have no idea of what A.A. is actually like. Or, they may dread the idea of association with "those people." Some who are well aware of their own alcoholic state feel utterly hopeless, "too far gone for A.A. to help." Even if they are not low-bottoms, they may seriously doubt that A.A. can help them.

Only as we become fully aware of the look and feel of the alcoholic's world can we appreciate how difficult it is to reach the person—to establish a line of communication.

And only as we grasp the changes which have occurred in the course of becoming alcoholic can we comprehend the scope of the changes which "recovery" will require. So much of the person's field has changed that just to quit drinking is not enough. This is pointed up sharply by the experience of one alcoholic who, before coming into A.A., had managed to stay "dry" for a whole year:

I was dry—off the booze—for one year by myself, and by myself I was! I was all alone. I had no social contacts with anybody. I was isolated from the world, so to speak. I went home from work every night terrified. I didn't know what to do with myself, so I would eat supper and I would be in bed by 7:30 or 8:00 o'clock, and that would alleviate the problem of sitting there watching television or thinking about having a drink. It was a very miserable, lonely way of life. I still had all my "character defects." I hated everybody. I resented all different types of things. (35-M-2/6)

As A.A.'s would say, this man was "dry" but did not have "sobriety." A.A.'s believe that real recovery requires more than taking drinking out of one's life. The entire field, which was changed so much while the drinking became central, needs to undergo substantial changes before the person can comfortably and happily live without drinking.

But this situation constitutes an apparently insoluble dilemma. As long as the alcoholic keeps drinking, the needed field changes cannot occur, and the person cannot keep from drinking, for long, unless the other changes do occur. It is no wonder that most alcoholics never find their way out of this "Catch-22" trap.

Full awareness of this dilemma helps us to appreciate not only the long-run solution which is inherent in the A.A. program and way of life, but also the manner in which the newcomer is enabled to make a start on the road toward the solution. Anyone who has dealt with alcoholics knows that reaching the trapped alcoholic is no mean achievement. How then does A.A. reach the new person and help in the touch-and-go job of beginning the process of change? Let us see what we can learn from A.A. members who describe their first contacts with A.A.

I had determined that I was hopeless, and there was nothing I could do about it. There is no way to explain the feelings within you when you get to that state. You are so completely at a loss. You don't understand yourself, and others don't understand you. You have lost all faith in yourself—all belief in yourself and in anyone else. It is a completely hopeless state. At that first meeting, the one thing I really grabbed hold of was hope—and the fact that several of the individuals were friendly. I believe that while I enjoyed the meeting and heard a lot that made sense, I think I would have gotten up and walked out of that meeting if some of those men hadn't come around and made me a very warm welcome. I think that was the clincher. I had not yet learned about the program, but it was enough at that time to know that apparently it worked. (Male)

I went to my first meeting considerable laced with wine because I was terrified. I didn't know what I was going to find. I don't remember who the speakers were or what they said. Having believed that there was no chance that I could ever stop drinking—and convinced that I was going to die and that there was nothing that I could do about it—I left the meeting with a feeling of hope. I also felt that these were people who cared, which was a kind of new feeling for me because I never felt like anybody really cared. (42-F-0/6)

What stands out in the two accounts is the arousal of *hope*—communicated in the most convincing manner possible, namely, by the flesh and blood example of persons who had found their way out of helplessness and hopelessness. Important also were the *friendly and caring attitudes* about which more will be said as we go on.

A major impact of the first A.A. meeting, for many, is the discovery that they are *not unique*—that others have the same problem. For some, this is an astounding revelation:

I was still upset, nervous and sick when I attended my first meeting—a large meeting with quite a few women there. I was overwhelmed. All I can remember was not the speaker, but the people. I looked at the women. One I figured was a social worker and the others must be the wives or relatives of the alcoholics, I thought I was the only woman drunk there, and it was absolutely unbelievable when these women came over to me and told me they were alcoholics. It was really like a ton of bricks off my head, knowing that there were other women who drank and got drunk—mothers like I was. That's really all I remember except that I saw love and something there that I wanted. (40-F-6/11)

I really don't remember too much about the first meeting, but I was surprised that the group looked as good as it did, and that I really wasn't that unique. (28-M-0/5)

The first wonderful thing in A.A. that was opened to me was that there were millions like me and that it wasn't something to be ashamed of because there was something that could be done about it. (Male)

Others were pleasantly surprised and greatly relieved to find that the members they saw there were *not at all like stereotypes* they had held of A.A. people:

Before coming into A.A., I had the impression that A.A. was nothing more than a bunch of drunks holding each other up, and I didn't want to be a part of it. It was despicable, just as bad as my drinking. My ideas were changed in the treatment center, and when I attended my first meeting outside, I found warmth, I found love, and I found acceptance. (43-M-1/2)

I had the idea that A.A. was for real old people, Skid-Row-type drunks—a bunch of old men sitting around, dirty, coffee dripping down their shirts, etc. But when I walked into my first A.A. meeting, taken there by an A.A. woman who had called on me, I was the only dirty one there. Everybody greeted me with open arms. I was still shaking because I was coming off a drunk. Yet everybody was so very helpful. They didn't make me feel ashamed. They made me feel that everything was going to be all right. I just felt at home there. (44-F-18/10)

I can't remember much of what was said at my first A.A. meeting other than the impression that the roomful of people gave me. They were laughing and they were talking and they were all clear-eyed. I still couldn't imagine anybody laughing and having a good time without a couple of hookers under the belt. (63-F-21/6)

Humor and *laughter* are striking characteristics of A.A. meetings generally. But of all the favorable first impressions about A.A., it is the *friendliness* of the people which leads the list—their *warmth*, their *acceptance*, and their *concern*:

My first A.A. meeting was a closed discussion meeting. I cannot recall the subject that was discussed on that particular evening. What stands out in my memory about that meeting is the people—the friendliness—the way they had of welcoming you and making you feel that you were in the right place. (32-M-0/7)

I didn't know anything about A.A. before coming into A.A. I really had no idea, either negative or positive. I don't remember much about that first meeting. It is all very blurred, very vague. There were a lot of people, and they were very nice to me; but I didn't know what they were talking about because I was very mixed up. But I liked it. I liked the people being friendly and taking my hand and remembering my name. (53-F-5/10)

At my first A.A. meeting, I remember everybody was happy, telling jokes, acting just like you would like to have people act anywhere else. I was irritated about this at first because I thought this should be almost like church—a serious place. Everybody is a "found-out drunk," and you're suppose to be hashing over this problem. But the people seemed to be happy, and the strangest thing about it all was that they were shaking my hand and being friendly to me. This was new for me. It was just out of this world. (37-M-2/7)

Very often, it is *one particular person* at the first meeting who makes a big difference:

At my first meeting, my hands were shaking like a leaf. I had reached the point where I was afraid of crowds, and I almost panicked when I walked into this room. But the people looked happy and friendly. Then a woman asked me if I wanted a cup of coffee. I panicked because I knew I couldn't hold the cup without spilling it. She put her hand on my arm, and she looked in my eyes and said, "I will hold it for you." When I looked in her eyes, I knew she understood. (32-F-4/0)

At my first meeting, after I came back to A.A., we were sitting around a table. When my time came, I told them I had been in A.A. many years before. Then a guy leaned across the table and smiled at me and grabbed my hand and said, "Welcome home." I had a feeling of being accepted for the first time in many years. (53-M-7/11)

My first A.A. meeting was a speaker-type, led by an alcoholic priest. That impressed me the most—that a priest was an alcoholic. Why should I be so ashamed to be an alcoholic? And I was impressed by the fact that he was so friendly, and he talked to me after the meeting for about 20 mintues. And he told me that if he could do it (achieve sobriety) I could too—one day at a time. (52-M-2/6)

The first meeting I attended, this time around when it stuck, was a large speaker meeting. And the strongest impression I got of that was that, this time, someone bothered to come over and to introduce himself to me, to take an interest in me personally on a one-to-one basis, and to follow up the meeting with a phone call, and who kept following up to the point where I become more involved in A.A. than I had been the first time. (41-M-1/2)

Another dynamic factor in initially reaching the alcoholic newcomer is what A.A. members call *identifying*. Many prospects come to A.A. with their fingers crossed—still doubting that they are alcoholics—or doubting that they and the "A.A. people" have enough in common. But, when the newcomer hears speakers tell about experiences and feelings like his own, the newcomer identifies with the speaker. He comes to feel he *is* among others like himself—that he *is* where he belongs:

I was taken to my first meeting by my first sponsor. She introduced me to everybody—everybody shook my hand. The two speakers were men. I can't remember now what they said, but their lives in their teens and twenties, things they had done, I identified with them right away. In fact, I laughed and sat there and howled. I had done similar things even though I was a woman. They did leave an impression on me. I was still shaky, but I was glad I went, really surprised to see all these people. They were all dressed casually, and they had plenty of coffee, and they could hold a cup of coffee. Everybody was so darn nice, and that made a good impression. I wasn't afraid. (55-F-3/4)

At my first meeting I was amazed to hear all these people talking about fears and problems that I had had and had never talked to anybody about. It gave me a feeling of being very comfortable. I felt like I had arrived at a place where I was very much at home and that these people knew what they were talking about. They had all gone through the mill that I had. I had a very comfortable feeling being there. (35-M-2/6)

My first meeting was a discussion meeting. I heard people talking about denting fenders on their automobiles, getting divorces, and beating their children, and I thought "My God, I've never done these things." But the thing that stuck in my mind more than anything else was someone's mentioning the blackout. I asked, "What do you mean?" They said this is a period of time which you can't remember. I said, "My God, I have been having them for years." I had gotten into a lot of trouble through the years. I would make promises to people and never keep them— and they would say, "Don't you remember you said this?" and I'd have to say that I can't remember. I guess I identified more with the blackout than anything else. (47-M-8/10)

Early on, A.A.'s recognized that newcomers will not identify with every member who speaks. Accordingly, the custom developed at speaker meetings to have two or three speakers and a leader who also works in some of his own story before and between speakers. Almost always, at least one of the speakers is a woman. The functionality of this custom of multiple speakers is pointed up in the following accounts:

I didn't like the idea of coming to A.A. for help. The first speaker was a robust, typical heavy drinker, a type of drinker I could not identify with at all. As a matter of fact, after listening to him I didn't think I was in the right place. However, the second speaker was a woman who had a drinking pattern very similar to mine. She also came from a family of nondrinkers and drank very little while in college. But her drinking got underway and progressed during her twenties. So I was able to identify with her very quickly—which got me very interested in A.A. and kept me coming back to hear some more about this. (41-M-5/10)

At my first meeting, I heard some stories that told me that this was not the place for me. But then the leader of the meeting stood up, and I felt he was talking about me. It angered me, and I even charged that somebody had gotten a phone call from one of my family who had told them every bad thing I had done while I was drinking. That was not true, but I see now that what really happened was that I had completely identified with an alcoholic who had the same feelings and experiences that I had. (48-M-8/4)

Sometimes, a newcomer's first A.A. meeting may be that of a group which has no one with whom he or she can identify— or a group in which the newcomer cannot feel at home. In the two following cases, the persons later did become involved in A.A., but they were turned off by their first meeting:

My first meeting had an open speaker meeting, and it took me one half-hour before I even had the courage to go in the building. I didn't know what to expect. A woman speaker told about hiding bottles and drinking in a very strange way. I didn't identify at all with her. I didn't believe that I had a problem, but I knew she did! But when I went to a treatment center about 3 years later and attended an A.A. meeting, it was different. I saw something in the people: they looked happy, and that was something I wanted but didn't know how to get. (39-M-0/9)

My first meeting was in a home, mostly men and only four women. I was afraid I couldn't relate to the men because their experiences would not at all be like mine. But I couldn't relate to the women either. The language I heard was frightening, and I really thought that maybe I had made a mistake, like I wasn't going to fit in there. The next day I called the minister-counselor I knew, and he put me in touch with a woman he thought I could relate to. That was good. She is still my sponsor, and she's great. At the time, she introduced me into other groups where I felt more at home. But since then, I have gone back to the original group, and I like it. (52-F-0/4)

Even though it does not always happen, it is general A.A. practice to try to arrange congenial first contacts. Also, when other groups are available nearby, the newcomer is generally taken to, or advised to attend, the meetings of a variety of groups and then to join the one to which he or she feels most attracted—feels most at home.

Up to this point we have been touching upon significant aspects of the A.A. social environment—as seen through the eyes of newcomers to A.A. But, as suggested in the following account, there is still more to the atmosphere of a typical A.A. group:

> My first A.A. meeting was a mixed group, about 30 persons there, and my greatest impressions were these: one, that I was definitely in a roomful of drunks—just the way they talked, their mannerisms, and so on. I remember almost wondering when someone was gonna bring out the booze. The other impression was that I just could not believe the level of acceptance I saw there. I had never seen such accepting people in my life—of each other, not just me. There were very warm good feelings—in a way, like coming home. (38-M-0/3)

In this account, we have our attention called to two very significant and distinctive qualities of the A.A. social environment: (1) the *verbal* and *nonverbal language* and (2) the *high level* of acceptance.

We will have more about A.A. language, its functions, its special words, phrases, and the special meanings given certain common terms. But, we now note the role of language in reaching the alcoholic newcomer. In the above account "the way they talked, their mannerisms" left no doubt in this man's mind that he was among authentic boozers—so much so that he almost expected the booze to be brought out any minute. What individual newcomers hear and see in an A.A. meeting will not always be such a perfect match with their own past drinking surroundings, but the fact that they are among "real drunks" will nevertheless be obvious.

Another general characteristic of A.A. language—both as spoken and as used in all A.A. literature—is that it is the simple, everyday language which people generally use. Technical or professional words are avoided, or if used, are generally employed in their ordinary, lay sense ("ego" for example). Such language is highly functional in that it connects with the widest range of persons. It also facilitates communication at an *emotional* as well as at an intellectual level—what A.A.'s call the "language of the heart."

As for the *high level* of acceptance, this man found it difficult to believe that such a quality of acceptance could exist in any human group. Furthermore, he found this attitude to be shown not just to newcomers but toward each other. This does not mean, of course, that every member learns to like every other member. By no means. A.A. members are busy being human, too. But I do agree that the overall quality of acceptance is remarkably high. And I believe that this "acceptingness" is a major factor in reaching the newcomer. In fact, I hold that it is also a major factor in personal growth—in the continuing progress of members toward emotional health.

What makes for such a quality of acceptance? For one thing, *having a common problem*—and not just an ordinary one but a kind of life-and-death problem—makes it possible to understand each other and to *empathize* to a degree nonalcoholics find difficult to comprehend. Even members who have not been in the program long and/or have not emerged very far out of their egocentric shell, they are nevertheless able to empathize with another alcoholic.

Also making for acceptance is the A.A. emphasis upon *honesty* and the resulting *openness* with which the members talk about their own unacceptable, but typical, past behavior and feelings. So often, after hearing a member tell his story, it is as if one has known that person well for years. The particular speaker may still have unlikable characteristics, but the listener has now become aware of that member's background and some of the experiences which account, at least in part, for his present personality and behavior. A basic human bond has been established—a bond which spells acceptance of this person as another struggling, fellow human being. When we take note of all the one-to-one lines of "fellow feeling" among A.A.'s we can see why "fellowship" is the term A.A.'s use to describe their society.

Certainly, the qualities of empathy, honesty, openness, and acceptance—so abundantly present in the A.A. social environment—are major, dynamic factors in A.A.'s effectiveness.

Furthermore, these qualities are strongly supported by two basic, normative ways in which A.A. members relate to each other: (1) *as equals*, and (2) *with respect for each other's autonomy*.

Of all the self-help/mutual-help *peer* groups now in existence none exceeds A.A. in terms of real equality. There are no authority figures in local A.A. group life or anywhere in the fellowship, as we shall see when we sketch A.A.'s overall structure (Chapter 10). At all levels, the norm in A.A. is to operate on the group dynamics principle of *shared leadership*.

A striking attitude which functions to support equality is the *basic respect for the dignity and autonomy of each individual*. I recall my surprise when I first heard a member reflect this attitude with the statement: "You know, when anyone comes into this group, he still retains his right to go out and get drunk." At the time, I thought this was going a little too far, but I came to appreciate the importance of this total respect for the autonomy and integrity of the individual.

Alcoholics are particularly "allergic" to having others telling them what to do. A.A. members know this from their own experience and are especially careful not to preach—or not to pressure the newcomer (or not to pressure each other, later on). A.A. does have a program and a way of life, but individuals are given the freedom to move along at their own pace. The phrase, "There are no 'musts' in A.A." is meant to speak to this point. The Twelve Steps constitute a *suggested* program of recovery. The Steps are prefaced with "Here are the steps we took" not "Here are the steps you must take." Newcomers will eventually learn that solid recovery means the practice of all Twelve Steps—the *entire* A.A. program, but members are free to proceed at their own speed.

One of the most striking aspects of this respect for autonomy is leaving it up to the individual to make his own diagnosis—to decide whether or not he or she is an alcoholic. The members share their own experiences, and they show understanding and caring, but it is up to the individual to apply these shared experiences to himself.

This makes A.A.'s approach very soft-sell—very permissive—in contrast to the aggressive, confrontational approach of some other group programs. When we call to mind the alcoholic's distortion of reality, the serious dilemma in which he is trapped, and his difficulty in even recognizing his alcoholism, it might seem too risky to leave the diagnosing up to the alcoholic himself. But the first A.A.'s found out that a diagnosis made by another person had little impact on the rationalizing, denying alcoholic. They learned that in this difficult step the newcomer must himself arrive at this conviction. Otherwise, fingers remain crossed.

However, A.A. does provide a climate—a total environment—which makes this self-diagnosis possible—and facilitates it.

Because it is such a difficult and big step, let us turn to a closer examination of the process by which a variety of A.A. members first came to *recognize*, then *admit*, and finally *accept* the reality of their alcoholism.

FIVE

"I Am An Alcoholic"

One of the first things to strike a visitor at an A.A. meeting is the manner in which A.A. speakers introduce themselves. For example, Joe will get up there and say, "My name is Joe, and I am an alcoholic." In most geographic areas, the audience will respond with a warm and sometimes vigorous, "Hi, Joe."

One A.A. man recalls his first reaction to this:

What stands out most in my memory of my first meeting was the surpirse of hearing the first guy that got up and talked. He said he was an alcoholic, and I was surprised that he admitted this right in front of all those people. I thought he didn't have much character left, and so on. I had my own image of what an alcoholic was, and I didn't think he fitted. Then I found out that all the speakers got up and said they were alcoholics, and I found out that I was in a roomful of drunks.

"I am an alcoholic." This self-identification raises a number of questions. Why do A.A. members identify themselves as alcoholics? What are the functions of such a self-designation? What does it usually take to bring alcoholic men and women to *recognize*, *admit*, and then fully *accept* the reality that they are alcoholics?

The newcomer will discover that A.A. members spend little time on analyzing why a person becomes alcoholic. *A.A.'s focus is on recovery.* And because this is the focus, thinking about the possible past causes of an individual's alcoholism is not considered to be relevant to initiating the process of recovery. In fact, on the basis of collective experience, newcomers are even cautioned against spending time trying to pinpoint the particular reasons why they took to drinking and why they became alcoholics. Intellectualizing along this line is held to be not only unprofitable but, at least at first, is seen as actually diverting attention from the main task at hand. In one of A.A.'s succinct phrases, the counsel to the newcomer is, "Don't analyze—utilize."

For the newcomer, the first important task is a *realistic appraisal* of the *present* state of affairs. This is the vital, initial focus. And it is this realistic appraisal that the members are ready to help the new person make. As I have indicated, this is done not by making the appraisal for the new man or woman, but rather by offering their own experiences, their time, and their caring support.

For the new person, making a realistic appraisal of his or her present condition requires an honest answer to the very difficult question, "Am *I* an alcoholic?" Usually, this requires some "de-stereotyping"—a clear view of what an alcoholic is.

As I indicated earlier, A.A.'s model of an alcoholic is the same as Jellinek's gamma type, exhibiting a double loss of control: not only the ability to control *when* he will drink, but also *how much* he will drink once started.

However, A.A. does not use a formal definition. A.A. has its own language to describe the condition. First of all, the alcoholic is said to have an illness, a disease. While A.A. did not originate the disease concept, A.A.'s adoption of the health frame has been fundamental to its success.

As for the nature of this illness, the first of the A.A. Twelve Steps[1] comes right to the point in first-person, experiential terms: "*We admitted we were powerless over alcohol—that our lives had become unmanageable.*"

This step constitutes the realistic appraisal of the alcoholic newcomer's plight. However, as we have emphasized, this is a self-diagnosis the acceptance of which is usually resisted—often strenuously—by persons in whose lives alcohol has become central in the management of living.

In view of this resistance and in view of the commonly held stereotypes of what an "alcoholic" is, the phrase "powerless over alcohol" is well chosen. As Joan Jackson[2] has pointed out, the phrase communicates the hard truth in language which is free of the "social, emotional and punitive overtones of words like 'helpless,' 'unable to control,' 'weak-willed,' etc., with which the idea has been cloaked in the past." The wording, she points out, "allows the core idea to stand clear" so that it can be thought about in a new way.

We should also note the further choice of words used by Bill and the early A.A.'s to describe the nature of this powerlessness over alcohol. It consists of a "mental obsession" and an "allergy of the body."

"Mental obsession" well describes the powerful, compulsive relationship to alcohol previously described—a relationship which makes it virtually impossible to give up drinking, for long, without help.

---

[1] The Twelve Steps, constituting what A.A.'s call their "recovery program," are given in full on pages 90–91.

[2] Joan K. Jackson, *A Second Look at Alcoholics Anonymous*, unpublished paper.

The reader will have no trouble with "mental obsession," but why "allergy of the body"?

"Allergy" was first used by Dr. William Silkworth,[3] to describe the abnormal physical condition which he believed made it impossible for Bill and others like him to control the extent of drinking once started. This fitted Bill's experience and that of the other early A.A. members. Speaking of them, Bill wrote:

It did not satisfy us to be told that we could not control our drinking just because we were maladjusted to life, that we were in full flight from reality, or were outright mental defectives. These things were true to some extent, in fact, to a considerable extent with some of us. But we are sure that our bodies were sickened as well. In our belief, any picture of the alcoholic which leaves out this physical factor is incomplete.

(*Alcoholics Anonymous*, p. xxiv)

This statement sums up the view among A.A.'s which still prevails. What this physical factor is called is quite secondary. Allergy is still used by many A.A.'s today, although less frequently. If used, it may be used literally or as an analogy: "like an allergy." One often hears the terms "physical sensitivity" or "X-factor" used instead. It is recognized among A.A.'s that scientists have not yet determined what the physical X-factor or factors may be.

No matter what our own view may be, we can recognize that "allergy" is a *functionally useful* term, whether used with or without quotation marks. It points to a real and serious condition, the inability to control how much one will drink. Referring to the condition as an allergy makes it easier to

[3] William D. Silkworth, M.D., was the medical director of Towns Hospital, a New York facility which treated alcoholics and at which Bill W. was under Dr. Silkworth's personal care in 1934 (see "The Doctor's Opinion" in *Alcoholics Anonymous*, 3rd ed, pp. xxiii-xxx).

accept and to act accordingly. If a person is allergic to strawberries, it is nothing to be ashamed of. It is a difference which one accepts. One simply cuts out eating strawberries. Thus, allergy suggests a new and useful way of looking at the distressing inability to control how much one drinks.

Turning back to the repetitive designation of oneself as an alcoholic, we may wonder why A.A.'s keep repeating this stigmatized label. Does this not perpetuate the negative identity which would better be left behind?

There are a number of things to be said about this practice which, like almost everything else in A.A., grew out of experience. For one thing, the constant repetition helps to destigmatize the term. When everyone in the new social environment openly wears the label, the term gradually loses its sting for the newcomer.

But, more important, "alcoholic" soon ceases to be a negative identity and becomes instead a *positive*, *hopeful NEW identity* which has three very basic and constructive functions:

1. Being alcoholic explains so much of the baffling and distressing *past*.
2. Understanding what "being alcoholic" is greatly changes the *present*—reduces confusion, anxiety, and guilt—and displaces despair with hope.
3. Understanding, admitting, and finally fully accepting the new identity becomes the very basis for handling and changing the *future*.

The new identity as an alcoholic cuts right through all the confusion, through all the rationalizations and denials to the two basic aspects of being "powerless over alcohol." At the same time, the new identity clearly reveals the courses of action to take. First, an alcoholic (the type A.A.'s are talking about and as A.A.'s see it) has permanently lost the ability to drink in a safe and controlled manner. Course of action?

Drinking must be given up altogether. Second, an alcoholic cannot give up drinking on a permanent basis unless freedom is won from the mental obsession which impells him or her to resume drinking despite the most earnest intentions not to. Course of action? One by which the mental obsession with drinking can be dissolved. A.A. offers a program of action which, if followed, will bring about this freedom.

Living without alcohol and *getting rid of the mental obsession*—as impossible as these changes appear to be at first—are nevertheless the clear-cut, logical imperatives for achieving solid sobriety. Every time a member says, "I am an alcoholic," these twin imperatives are acknowledged. And when a member who has been "in the program" with some length of sobriety still says, "I am an alcoholic," he or she is in effect saying that the inability to drink with control is still present and always will be, even though freedom from the obsession has been gained.[4]

But we should add that when the member with some length of sobriety says "I am an alcoholic," he is also acknowledging that continued freedom from the "mental obsession" is contingent upon continuing to grow in the new orientation to his world—continuing to grow in healthy ways of thinking and feeling about himself, about others, and about life. He is

---

[4] What about the proposition that some alcoholics can be returned to controlled (moderate, nonproblem) drinking? I have followed the findings with regard to this question. They indicate that a very small number of apparently gamma alcoholics has been able to return to controlled drinking. However, to date, it has *not* been demonstrated that controlled drinking is a feasible goal for treatment programs for gamma alcoholics. (For the follow-up to the most widely published controlled drinking study, see Pendery et al., 1982.) Abstinence is still the only practical and safe treatment goal.

This is also the perspective of alcoholism treatment centers. As stated by Bissell and Deakins (1978), "We do not deny the fact that an occasional alcoholic has been able to return to social drinking. In the view of the fact, however, that no one has as yet been able to identify this rare individual in advance and that a wrong guess may well cost the patient his life, we are firm in insisting on abstinence as the goal of therapy."

acknowledging that the old alcohol-centered ways of thinking and feeling are never completely extinguished. But he is also indirectly affirming that by association with others who are learning and growing in the new way of life, and by taking the actions called "working the steps" or "working the program," the new orientation which gives freedom from the obsession will become increasingly dominant.

However, our major concern in this chapter is with the initial step of making—and fully accepting—the realistic appraisal of being alcoholic. This is an extremely important step, for without this clear-cut assessment and its acceptance at the "gut level," the alcoholic does not yet have a firm footing in reality. But we should also add that, for most alcoholics, this is a difficult step to take.

Because this step is so difficult and so basic, it is worthwhile listening to what a variety of A.A.'s have to say about their own experiences in coming to this self-appraisal; also what these members reveal about the A.A. environment which helped them to *see, admit*, and *accept* the reality of being alcoholic.

The following three accounts provide a general perspective:

It took me a long time to accept that I was an alcoholic. I admitted that I was, but it is another thing to accept and believe that I was an alcoholic. I think I was in A.A. maybe as long as 8 months before I really felt comfortable speaking out about my problem and accepting that I was a person that just couldn't handle booze. A big help was learning that I was just a person who had a disease—one that could be arrested—so, therefore, it just wasn't that terrible. (35-M-2/6)

I admitted that I was an alcoholic the day before I went to A.A. I admitted it but I didn't know what an alcoholic was. I knew that I had a problem with alcohol, but I really did not want to quit drinking. I only wanted to quit drinking so much. It was not until I had been on the program a few weeks that I found out what being alcoholic really meant and that I really was an alcoholic. (58-M-20/0)

It took a while to admit that I was an alcoholic. Frankly, I did not think I was an alcoholic, even after being in A.A. for a number of weeks. It is obvious to me now that I didn't know what an alcoholic was. I did admit right at the beginning that I had a drinking problem and that the program would do me no harm. But it was only after a number of weeks of attending meetings that I realized that I had done the same things that the others who identified themselves as alcoholics had done. My drinking patterns were the same, and my life was heading in the same direction. So, by these two identifications, I determined that I was an alcoholic. (41-M-5/10)

Another member who had been attending meetings quite regularly and associating with A.A. members said he didn't like admitting he was an alcoholic and that his doing so was a kind of intellectual statement made in order to participate in A.A. activities. Then, he revealed the *three prerequisites* to his eventual acceptance—three factors which together made acceptance possible and which, I believe, apply to most A.A. members:

I accepted the fact that I was an alcoholic when I found out what an alcoholic was, when I became honest enough to realize that this was my problem, and when I came to feel that it was no longer necessary to drink. (54-M-12/0)

The above accounts illustrate the recognition among A.A.'s that there is usually a considerable difference between the *admission* and the *acceptance* of being an alcoholic. Even *admitting* being an alcoholic can mean different things unless the person making the statement has acquired a clear concept of what an alcoholic is. Most alcoholics, when they come to A.A. or to a treatment facility, have confused or partial concepts of what an alcoholic is. Education or clarification on this point is a necessary foundation for making a realistic appraisal.

The words will be there in almost every first A.A. contact: "Powerless over alcohol"—"disease"—"illness"—"a physical condition coupled with a mental obsession." But the big question is personal—painfully personal, "Am *I* an alcoholic?" So it is not surprising that not many coming to A.A. (or to help of any kind) are able to make this self-diagnosis quickly. However, here are two who did:

I knew that I had a drinking problem because once I started I couldn't stop. There were also circumstances and events which had driven me down. So, I admitted I was an alcoholic at that first meeting. I would say that I accepted the fact just as soon as I understood the first step. That was in about ten days. (64-F-26/1)

I accepted the fact that I'm an alcoholic the very first night. I came home from my first meeting with the Big Book that I was given, and I sat up all night and read it. And, from that time on, I've never questioned the fact that I'm an alcoholic. It was immmediate acceptance. (42-F-3/7)

Then there are some for whom the alcoholic identity actually comes as a big relief. For example, this was the reaction of the man who, at his first meeting, had learned what a blackout was:

I recall leaving the meeting. I got in my car and started to drive home. I remember exactly where I was driving. All of a sudden it occurred to me—and I said it out loud: "I am an alcoholic!" I felt as though a weight had been lifted from my shoulders because I had been believing that a lot of this loss of memory had to do with losing my mind. (47-M-8/10)

In another instance, a 47-year-old middle-class woman who had been incarcerated after her second drunk-driving arrest found great relief in learning at her first A.A. meeting that she was an alcoholic, that she had an illness and was "not a bum." She was "so grateful."

Alcoholic? Powerless over alcohol? For most who come to A.A. still anchored in their distorted world of rationalization and denial, the meaning and implications of this reality are difficult to comprehend and to apply honestly to themselves. It is only gradually, as they listen to other A.A. members telling about how it had been with them, that are they able to grasp their own situation.

Even as they listen, there are those who listen very selectively at first. As they listen to speakers, they hope to discover that they are not alcoholics. They pay more attention to the differences than to the similarities:

Three years before I came back into A.A., under some pressure from home and the job, I started attending some meetings. But I didn't believe I was an alcoholic. There were all these "I nevers"—things that had happened to the speakers but not to me. I'd never lost a wife, a family, a job, wrecked cars or been in jail. But in the two-week period before I came back into A.A., these "I nevers" happened. I was thrown out of the house, almost lost my job, did crash up a car. I was a physical wreck, shaking and sweating at work. I finally accepted the fact that I was an alcoholic when these things all happened. I was literally killing myself. I just wanted to live. (51-M-3/0)

I continued going only to open meetings. I was mouthing the words that I was an alcoholic, yet in the back of my mind I was saying maybe I'm not; and I was looking for reassurance from the people that I really wasn't an alcoholic. Then I started going to the closed meetings. When I finally stopped comparing, things started to hit home. It became clear that I had such an obsession for a drink that the normal, average person does not have, and that is what really convinced me that I was an alcoholic. (32-F-0/6)

I was in the A.A. program about 9 months before I could admit I was an alcoholic. I really did not like that word. At meetings, the speakers talked about what they had done, the jails that they had been in, the institutions, jobs they had lost.

I wasn't identifying with any of these things. One day, a guy said at a meeting that it wasn't the things that he had done that had caused him to come to A.A. and to realize that he was an alcoholic, but the things that he neglected to do as a result of his drinking. And from that day until today I have never had any problems in saying that I was an alcoholic. (44-F-18/w)

Because of this initial tendency to look for differences, the counsel to newcomers has been summed up in another simple phrase, "Don't compare—identify!" It is through identifying with the others that most newcomers to A.A. learn what an alcoholic is and become able to face up to the reality that this is what they are:

By listening to a lot of the people I heard speak I started to identify with them. I realized I was very similar to them, and if they were alcoholics, I was too. (39-M-0/9)

By the third meeting, I did admit I was an alcoholic because I could judge from the stories being told that I wasn't the only one that did these kooky things—hiding the bottles, the blackouts, and the whole thing. It was that early process of education—and finding out that I have a disease—that led me to admit I was an alcoholic. But it was another 4 months before I finally surrendered and accepted that I was an alcoholic. (50-M-3/0)

After attending quite a few meetings for approximately 6 months, and hitting about five meetings a week, it was by identifying with the speakers more than anything else that I came to admit that I, too, had a problem; then for the next 3 months, I gave it lip service by saying "I am an alcoholic." However, it took me approximately a year in A.A. before I really and truly accepted it in my heart. (59-M-19/6)

There are many who report that, even after being in A.A., it *took more drinking* to convince them that they were indeed powerless over alcohol. The first of the following three accounts also describes the understanding with which A.A.'s accept this fairly common behavior:

> Unfortunately, it took more drinking. I had to prove to myself that I could not control it. For me, it took more drinking because I didn't have too many glaring symptoms when I came in. Despite this, the people still cared about me and supported me and kept calling. They didn't give up. Even after I had a few slips, they kept calling. (44-F-2/11)

> I admitted that my life was unmanageable through the use of alcohol. This I did when I called A.A. after a week-long debauch- er. My self-image had gone down, and I was nothing. I was a bum, all due to alcohol. But it was only after three slips during my first year in A.A. that I finally admitted and accepted that I was powerless over alcohol and that no matter what I did I could not drink. (34-M-4/0)

> I think I really admitted to the alcoholism when I went to a psychiatrist who knew something about alcoholism. I came to A.A. about 4 years later, and it took probably the first 2 years in A.A. for me to accept being an alcoholic. This came after two long slips, about 5 months on one and 7 months on the other. I had come into the program as a high-bottom and became a low- bottom, just one step away from the streets, before I accepted the fact that I just could not drink. (37-M-2/7)

In A.A., much emphasis is placed upon *being honest with oneself*. This is an obvious requirement for any realistic self- appraisal. But after years of rationalization, denial, and self- deception, "getting honest" with oneself is not easy. It is no wonder that a specific gain in self-honesty is mentioned as significant in accepting the fact of being an alcoholic:

> It took a long time to admit even to myself that I was an alcoholic, and that came just before I went for treatment. Even then, I couldn't accept it. I got out of the treatment unit and got drunk again. I tried A.A. in a superficial manner and got drunk again. I thought I had tried A.A. and that it didn't work for me.

One day, I was alone in the house and I remembered that I had read that some people had trouble making it because they weren't honest. That fitted me. I went back to the hospital treatment unit and was able to accept being an alcoholic in about a month. (55-F-14/6)

The next account shows that *the honesty of others* played a major role in helping the woman become honest with herself about her alcoholism. In addition, the woman mentioned other aspects of the usual A.A. environment which contributed to her freedom to be honest:

I asked A.A. for help, and a couple of women came out to call on me. This was in the morning, and I was still pretty drunk. I agreed to attend their meeting that evening. During the day, I got three or four phones calls from people I had never met. They introduced themselves and just said, "Hang in there. You have friends. You are not alone." At the meeting, we sat around a table. Everybody looked so nice and clean. They didn't look like bums. And they were honest! When they asked me if I would like to say something, I came out with: "My name is Ann, and I am an alcoholic." I also blurted out: "I don't have to lie anymore." It was such a relief. . . . Then, in a few weeks, I was asked to go along on a Twelfth Step call on a woman who had been sober at that first meeting and had slipped. I had never seen anything like this before. I felt that I was watching a movie of myself. We took the woman to the hospital. I was very deeply affected by this. I think that for the first time, in my gut, I felt, "That's me! I've got this disease." This was the actual point when I really accepted the fact that I was an alcoholic. (47-F-3/3)

This honest sharing of experience, which goes on constantly in A.A., is a powerful factor in helping newcomers see through their illusions and become honest with themselves.

The last account also reveals one of the major functions of the basic A.A. activity of calling on alcoholics who want help.[5] Seeing the shape the other alcoholic is in sharpens up in vivid,

[5] "Twelfth Step calls"—see Step Twelve, Page 91.

flesh and blood terms what it really means to be powerless over alcohol. The full reality of their own lives comes into sharp focus. It is not merely seen. It is felt—deeply. "That's me!"

The reality of one's own alcoholic behavior and condition comes into focus in a great variety of ways, as we have seen. Here are some additional reports:

During my first year in A.A., I thought I had accepted the fact of being alcoholic. I came back to A.A. after the worst drunk of my life. I was in the DT's for a couple of weeks. I came back feeling very hopeless and very frightened and I was very sick. I remember the night that I did come back. It was a hot August Sunday, and I was talking to one of my A.A. friends I had known during my year of sobriety. I was struggling to look back on my life and admit that it really was in shambles because of alcohol, and there came a moment when I was able to say, "I'm powerless over alcohol." With that a tremendous weight was lifted from my shoulders. (37-M-9/11)

Realizing the absolute insanity of my drinking—the self-abuse that was involved in drinking—I think it was this coming into focus as I stayed away from a drink 24 hours at a time that put me securely into the program this last time. (35-M-1/5)

During the 10 months between the time I first started coming to A.A. and the time I was able to stop drinking, I had about ten short slips. Each time I would admit that I had a problem. But I accepted the fact that I was an alcoholic after my wife had left, and I still tried over a period of three weekends to drink normally and couldn't. (47-M-8/0)

One aspect of "deep-down" acceptance of one's alcoholism is coming to terms with the "lifetimeness" of the condition, as illustrated in the following account:

Admitting that I was an alcoholic was fairly easy thing for me to do. All the signs were there. I just never had read them as being alcoholic because I never had a real definition of what an alcoholic was. Once I had attended a few meetings and got the gist of what was going on, I readily admitted to myself and others that I was an alcoholic. Accepting was a different ball game. It was probably a few months into the program that I really accepted the fact that I was an alcoholic and wasn't going to find some way to be able to drink—or learn how to drink. As soon as I did say to myself that I couldn't drink anymore, it was easy. Up to then, the big thing in my mind was, "Here I am, only 25 years old, and I can't drink for the rest of my life?" That was incomprehensible. (Male)

Professionals working with persons who have become seriously disabled (e.g., persons who have been blinded or have become paraplegic) report the difficulty of, and stress the importance of, *accepting the permanence* of their condition. As long as a person fights the idea, resents it, or feels sorry for himself, there is no sound foundation on which to build the best future possible.

So it is with the alcoholic. A.A.'s recognize the great difficulty of a complete acceptance of a lifetime of not drinking. Therefore they reduce the newcomer's problem to manageable size by the simple concept of staying away from the first drink, *one day at a time*. But, sooner or later, it becomes clear that this means one day at a time forever.

Our accounts, in this chapter, point up some of the *main factors* in the A.A. environment which play a part in helping newcomers to A.A. recognize, admit, and accept their powerlessness over alcohol. We have also seen that persons vary in their resistance to this appraisal. For some, it is a very short step from admission to acceptance. For some, even admission takes time. For most, full acceptance takes quite a while. There are some, as shown in the following account, for whom even the word of acceptance falls short of describing their experience:

I had been sober in A.A. for 6 months, until the day my daughter was married. Of course, being an Irish father, I had to lead the band. I opened the bar at the country club. Well, that was one wedding! And I had to attend another wedding the following day, that of my wife's niece. Well, by the time this bout ended, I realized that the A.A. people knew what they were talking about. I was a very, very sick individual. I recall one particular morning getting up, and I just couldn't make any excuse for myself. In the past, I used to rationalize it, even to the point of being ridiculous. But this particular morning I couldn't find a single, honest excuse, and I had to surrender—not admit—not accept—I had to completely surrender that I was licked by alcohol, completely powerless over it. (61-M-3/3)

In this chapter, we have been reviewing the experiences of a variety of A.A. members in answering the two basic questions: "What is an alcoholic?" and "Am I an alcoholic?"

We have seen that it is from the honestly shared experiences of other A.A. members that the newcomer obtains the information necessary to answer the question of what an alcoholic is. This may be gained, in part, through reading the A.A. literature. But most of the information is usually received directly in speaker or discussion meetings, and in the many before-, after-, and between-meeting conversations.

Even more important than the information provided are the *attitudes* of the members toward newcomers which penetrate their defenses and make it possible to receive and apply the information to themselves. It is the unusually high degree of understanding, acceptance, empathy, and caring—so characteristic of the A.A. climate—which "gets through" first and enables the newcomers to assess themselves honestly and come to *believe* as well as say, "I am an alcoholic."

SIX
Saying "Yes" to Life

> Since coming to A.A. and stopping drinking, a whole new
> world had opened up for me. But it's really the other way around:
> a whole new me is opening up to life. . . . It's wonderful!
> (Woman speaking at an A.A. meeting)

Most basic in winning freedom from the obsession to drink, I
have been saying, is the acquiring of a new orientation to life—
a more functional and productive way of thinking and feeling
about one's self, about others, and about life in general.

In alcoholics, drinking becomes so completely woven into
their organization of life, so central in their "self-system," that
it cannot be rooted out by itself. The whole self-system must
undergo restructuring. This means basic changes throughout
the field—basic changes in *ideas*, *attitudes*, and *values*—basic
changes in the person's *sense of self*. The most fundamental
need of all, according to the A.A. approach, is a central shift in

"basic trust." This means a shift from a trusting relationship with alcohol and the egocentric self in which alcohol is central, toward a trusting relationship with *life*.

A trusting relationship with life means a nondefensive, outgoing, trusting relationship with other persons. It means a trusting of the nondefensive, positive aspects of one's own being. And inseparably, it means a trust in the supportive and creative forces of life itself, so variously and sometimes paradoxically conceptualized.

I do not know of a simpler or more correct way of describing the *direction* of these changes in trust—in basic orientation—than in the woman's statement above: "*opening up to life*." And what is more needed! We have seen that becoming alcoholic is a process of becoming more and more "closed to life"—of feeling more and more cut off from people—more and more cut off from life. There is increasing constriction, increasing emotional encapsulation. We have noted the eventual powerlessness over alcohol and the resultant inability to be in control of one's life. Certainly, if the person is to live and function in any satisfactory manner, the old orientation must yield to—give way to—a new basis of operation, one which opens the person to life.

How does the A.A. way make it possible for the shift in orientation to begin and proceed? The first A.A.'s, trying to describe their own experiences of change, used language acceptable to them, including the William James concept of "Power greater than ourselves." If a reader believes that such a conceptualization is beyond the pale of scientific and professional outlook, he or she is still urged to pay close attention to the experience behind the words. If the A.A. program is to be understood—not misunderstood—it is necessary for the reader to be, or become, aware of the *actual experience* or *experiences* to which the A.A. concepts are applied. Experience is the reality, not the language.

As I have pointed out before, A.A.'s favor lay terms and

ordinary language which enable them to talk about their experiences to the widest spectrum of alcoholic persons. A.A.'s also give each other the greatest freedom to develop their own understanding of a greater power. They would expect each reader to feel equally free to do the same, utilizing whatever metaphors will enable the reader to describe or conceptualize the experiences. But they would hope that each person observing A.A., and trying to understand it, will constantly be aware of the actual experiences—of the very real phenomena or dynamics—referred to by traditional "spiritual" conceptualizations.

The focus in this chapter therefore will be upon *experience*—upon the *changes which actually occur*, most particularly upon the *change in basic orientation* referred to in the first three steps of the A.A. program.[1] We have already discussed the First Step. But, it will be repeated here along with the Second and Third Steps because it is an integral part of the process described in three, interrelated steps.

1. We admitted we were powerless over alcohol—that our lives had become unmanageable.
2. Came to believe that a Power greater than ourselves could restore us to sanity.
3. Made a decision to turn our will and our lives over to the care of God *as we understood Him*.

This is the language. What is the nature of the experience— the process—the reality—summed up in these steps? What can we observe?

One common obstacle to communication and understanding in this area lies in the very word "self." Our language simply does not have generally accepted terms to distinguish among the several ways in which we use "self." The most common confusion is to think of one's "self" (self-concept, self-system)

[1] The Twelve Steps in their entirety are to be found on pages 90–91.

as being the same as one's "*total* being." The two are not the same and the distinction is vital.

We have noted all along that the self which a given alcoholic person conceives himself to be becomes increasingly constricted. A therapist or objective observer knows that all kinds of capabilities, powers, and potentialities are nevertheless latent within the individual—both those the person had known before and those of which the person has never been aware. But these potentialities are *not now* a part of the self as known to the individual. From the viewpoint of the self—and that is all the individual can *believe* himself to be—such capabilities and potentialities are simple "not there." Certainly, they cannot be brought into the picture by any efforts or powers he calls his own. Accordingly, any hope of recovery depends upon some resources, some powers, greater than any that the individual can *believe* to be a part of the self he knows.[2]

Among the obvious, latent resources within the individual are energies presently blocked or burned-up by anxiety and inner conflicts, and potential energies presently unavailable because of serious neglect of health. There are blocked and unused conscious and unconscious mental powers. There are latent capacities to relate better to others, to love, give, and accomplish—that is, to be "productive" in the Erich Fromm sense of the word. These and other potentialities or "powers" are there. But to the alcoholic, they are anything but there. Consequently, to entertain the possibility of release from powerlessness, the alcoholic needs at least a glimmer of *hope*, tentative and partial though the belief may be, that "something greater," something more than self, is available to help him recover.

Many newcomers to A.A. begin by thinking of the A.A. group as their greater Power. Moreover, skeptical newcomers

---

[2] Relevant is John Mack's concept of "self-governance" and his insightful chapter on "Alcoholism, A.A., and the Governance of the Self" (1981).

are encouraged to begin with belief in *anything greater than themselves* which they are able to conceive, whether it be the group, the meetings, the program, the power of good—in fact, *anything* at all which is *more* than what the person can attribute to his own constricted self. It is impressive to observe the understanding, breadth, and tolerance with which this matter of something greater is handled among A.A. members. This freedom must certainly be one of the factors contributing to A.A.'s unfractured survival. There is no official view of a greater Power to be promoted. There are no arguments. It is expected that each person will develop his own conception of a greater or higher Power. It is believed that each person's developing experience will provide him with a personal basis for belief in something more than the limited self. Furthermore, it is believed that it is crucially important for each person's conception to be *his own*, consonant with his *own* experience.

A member is free to place his developing concept of a greater Power into a supernaturalistic or naturalistic framework. But, if he does the former, the chances are great that his past conception of "God" will undergo substantial revisions in the direction of a very personal Power—as illustrated in the following two reports:

I didn't know what the hell they were talking about when they mentioned the spiritual part of the program. I had always believed in a God, but it was a God sitting away up in the sky pointing a finger right at me and all the things that I had done wrong in my life. But since coming to A.A., I have discovered a very personal God. I prefer to call it my personal Higher Power. Now, this Power had been with me all my life, but I didn't know it and didn't know how to use it. (50-F-1/4)

I now feel God's presence. It is not as if He is up some place, away from me. He is not away from me, but is *with* me. This belief developed slowly, but it is real. And, with it, my fears went away. (40-F-3/10)

Returning to the first three Steps, we note that in Step One and Step Two we have two elements of the basic change in orientation: The recognition of personal powerlessness over alcohol and the unmanageability of one's life; and, in the second, *hope* that *a potential* for recovery does exist.

The third element in the basic-change process is described in the Third Step: "Made a decision to turn our wills and our lives over to the care of God *as we understood Him*." Together, these three steps are the foundation steps in the A.A. approach.

As paradoxical and baffling as all this may appear to some readers, particularly concerning Step Three, let me make the important point at the outset that what we are talking about here is a deep-down, *inner* shift in *trust* and *control*. It is not a shift from one neurotic dependency to another neurotic dependency—nor a shift to external control. Rather, it is an inner shift from a hopeless, alcoholic-centered, self-centered, closed-in orientation to a fresh orientation of *being open to life*. It is an *inner shift* from a defensive to a *growth* orientation—a shift from a negative to a *positive orientation to life*.

For a better understanding of the nature of this shift, let us turn to Harry M. Tiebout, M.D., the first psychiatrist to write about the dynamics inherent in the first three steps of the A.A. program—particularly about the role of *crisis* and *surrender*.

In his lecture at the 1950 Yale Summer School of Alcohol Studies, I heard Tiebout relate how he had learned, from some of his alcoholic patients in A.A., the value of a "hitting-bottom" crisis (a coming to the end of one's rope) and of the "surrender" of egocentric control. He stated, as he later wrote, that "surrender involved a deep shift in . . . emotional tone, not consciously willed but arising from changes in the unconscious psychodynamics, which caused the disappearance of one set of feelings and the emergence of another and very different set" (1961). He called the latter a "positive state," which he described in such affirmative terms as; a going-along-with feeling rather than struggling, fighting, and controlling; a live-and-let-live feeling; not being harassed by conscience problems; being more open-minded, more gentle and acceptant; able to share and participate; having a sense of inner peace.

Tiebout indicated that to him: "This change in the inner life was surprising at first. In time, it became evident not only that other A.A.'s went through the same kind of transformation or conversion but that unless they did, and retained it, their chances of remaining sober were minimal."

Tiebout also learned that, while this basic shift occurred suddenly in some cases (sometimes dramatically), the shift was a more gradual process in the vast majority (he estimated 90–95%). It was helped along by involvement of the person in the warm and accepting life of the A.A. group—helped along by hearing the experiences of others, and by becoming more honest and open as called for in the A.A. program.

But, whether suddenly or slowly, Tiebout concluded that it was not merely "hitting bottom" which produced the shift. It took the further act (although "not consciously willed") of surrendering the habitual, ego-centered control of one's life to release the inflow of a positive, constructive set of feelings—a positive state of mind. Hitting bottom was a precondition, but that had to be accompanied or followed by a "letting go" of the old basis of running one's life—letting go of the up-to-now vigorously defended but depleted "self-system."

After his lecture at Yale, I asked Tiebout what one surrenders *to*. He replied, "One does not surrender *to* anything. One just surrenders." But in his writings, I later noticed, he made clear that in surrendering one quits fighting the world and accepts *reality*; one gives in to "the constructive forces residing in every individual;" gives in to one's "own creative life forces." These powers, while shut out of the constricted self, are nevertheless *a given of life*. They are "there," potentially available; and—this is important—*can be counted on* to flow into the person's experience when and as he gives up trying to run his life on the old basis—when and as he abandons his defensive, egocentric position and quits trying to run his life from that embattled position.

Tiebout also made a distinction between the "*act* of surrender" and the "*state* of surrender." In doing so, he gave us a further clinical description of the surrender phenomenon. An act of surrender

is to be viewed as a moment when the unconscious forces of defiance and grandiosity actually cease effectively to function. When that happens, the individual is wide open to reality; he can listen and learn without conflict and fighting back. He is receptive to life, not antagonistic. He senses a feeling of relatedness and at-oneness which becomes the source of an inner peace and serenity, the possession of which frees the individual from the compulsion to drink. In other words, an act of surrender is an occasion wherein the individual no longer fights life, but accepts it. . . .

The emotional *state* of surrender [is] a state in which there is a persisting capacity to accept reality. . . in the active sense of reality being a place where one can live and function as a person acknowledging one's responsibilites and feeling free to make that reality more liveable for oneself and others. There is no sense of "must." Neither is there any sense of fatalism. With true unconscious surrender, the acceptance of reality means the individual can work in it with it. The state of surrender is really positive and creative. (Tiebout 1949)

We can perceive the positive inflow following surrender most clearly when a person's experiences build up to a decisive moment—a moment when strong resistance finally yields. This is well illustrated in the case of one of my earliest A.A. friends whom I'll call Mark.

Mark had been a heavy drinker for years, but managed to get

by. He had repeatedly gone on the wagon for a few months, once for a year, once for 14 months. But, 9 years before the final climax, he had begun morning drinking and from there on he would go on binges of 3 or 4 days at first, but eventually lasting up to a week or 10 days. During these years, he still believed that he could quit drinking on his own. When finally his wife could stand no more and said she was through, he went to A.A. He attended two meetings but felt that A.A.'s program was too simple. Besides, he rationalized, A.A. was for *uncontolled* drinkers and he had never "really tried" controlled drinking. This he now set out to do. When this serious attempt resulted in a 2-month binge, he realized "that the jig was up."

Mark described his feelings during his final drinking days. He had a great distrust of people. He seemed to be in a boat without oars or tiller—or like being out on the ocean with no stars in the sky to guide by. The world seemed all awry. He was full of alibis for not achieving. Only drink gave him the illusion of achieving. When he finally realized that his body could take no more drinking, when there were no longer any friends who could be tapped for $50, when his wife said she was through, when his final attempt at controlled drinking failed, he seemed to be completely cut off from everything and everybody—completely alone. He felt lost. It seemed to be the end of the trail. In his words, "All my ego defenses had collapsed." Nothing was left. An intense depression, lasting somewhere from 5 to 15 minutes, was experienced as being utterly alone in utter blackness. Then it seemed that a spotlight was turned on—and with it came the realization that he was still a human being, essentially good, and still having potentiality and that it was possible for this potentiality to be developed. Mark stated that in that moment of *self-realization* he seemed to *let go emotionally of all the "phoniness" of his previous organization of life*.

Mark later viewed the foregoing as the first phase of the

surrender experience. The second phase, he felt, was a *process of development*—an increasing realization of the essential goodness of life and his real self—a growing conviction that his inner attitudes and not the "world" had been the cause of his difficulties. There was also a growing awareness of a "divine will" which he referred to as "a rhythm of rightness;" and an increasing alignment of his will with this divine will—a going-along-with-life—which was facilitated by the recognition that what the egocentric Mark wanted was no longer important. He also read broadly and gave much thought to developing a satisfactory intellectual concept of a personal God, emotional attunement to which was the heart of his new orientation to life.

As a result of his own experience and that of many alcoholics he worked with in A.A., Mark concluded that the first three Steps in the A.A. program have to be taken together. The First Step cannot be taken alone, for by itself it is a hopeless step. The Second Step is the *hope*. The Third Step describes the "first inner shift" which follows as the result of the first two Steps. But, the Third Step is one which will have to be taken repeatedly until gradually there is a substantial consolidation of the new orientation.

Mark's account provides an excellent perspective on the experiences described in the first three Steps—as well as the quite typical events and feelings of the last drinking days. His experience also gives us a good example of Tiebout's findings with regard to surrender and the positive state which can be counted on to flow in when the person, feeling licked, gives up trying to run his life on a defensive, egocentric basis.

The following account reveals, in very condensed fashion, the same essential dynamics:

I didn't believe in God at all when I came into the program. . . . I thought my God had deserted me. When I was 2 weeks into the program, I was still suffering badly—suffering mentally, suffering physically, and I must have been suffering spiritually. I was lying in bed and my legs were cramped and I was sweating. I was in rotten shape. All I can remember is just sort of calling out: "If there is a God, for crying-out-loud, somehow show me." Well, I can't even describe it. It was like a warm, comforting feeling that came over me and said, "Allene, it will be all right." And I believed it. It was sort of incredible that I would believe it, but I did. (42-F-0/6)

Cofounder Bill W., when finally beaten down, had an experience like that of Mark's. The next day, to help him gain perspective on what had happened to him, he was given William James's classic, *Varieties of Religious Experience*. In Bill's words:

I devoured it from cover to cover. Spiritual experiences, James thought, could have objective reality; almost like gifts from the blue, they could transform people. Some were sudden brilliant illuminations; others came on very gradually. Some flowed out of religious channels; others did not. But nearly all had the great common denominator of pain, suffering, calamity. Complete hopelessness and deflation at depth were almost always required to make the recipient ready. The significance of all this burst upon me. *Deflation at depth*—yes, that was *it*. Exactly what had happened to me.[3]

"Deflation at depth"—or as Bill sometimes called it, "ego-deflation at depth"—this appeared to Bill (as it later did to Tiebout) to be the precondition for surrender, for turning to "more than self." And it is surrender which opens the person to the infusion of hitherto unsuspected power.

Bill's own experience and that of quite a few of the other early A.A.'s led them to stress the importance of such a spiritual experience. Bill's own story and that of many others

[3] *Alcoholics Anonymous Comes of Age*, pp. 63–64.

in the first printing of *Alcoholics Anonymous* (1939) left the impression on many alcoholic readers that a "spiritual experience" or a "spiritual awakening" (a term also used in the book) had to be "in the nature of sudden and spectacular upheavals." Many were discouraged by their failure to have such experiences. So the second printing, two years later (1941), included an appendix to provide a broader perspective. To quote in part:

Among our rapidly growing membership of thousands of alcoholics such transformations, though frequent, are by no means the rule. Most of our experiences are what the psychologist William James calls the "educational variety" because they develop slowly over a period of time. Quite often friends of the newcomer are aware of the difference long before he is himself. He finally realizes that he has undergone a profound alteration in his reaction to life; that such a change could hardly have been brought about by himself alone. . . . With few exceptions our members find that they have tapped an unsuspected inner resource which they presently identify with their own conception of a Power greater than themselves. (*Alcoholics Anonymous*, 1941, Appendix II.)

In other words—and this is supported by my own investigation—in the experience of most A.A. members, surrender comes in a series of what we might call smaller surrenders. Even when the first surrender is followed by an impressive shift in orientation, there remains the need for repeated surrenders until the new orientation becomes substantially consolidated—reasonably well established. But, whether major or minor, the surrenders are precipitated by some degree of "ego-deflation."

As I have indicated, A.A.'s are amazingly accepting of each other's conceptualizations of the greater or higher Power. Whether A.A. members conceptualize their own experience of the life-supporting and integrating forces in supernaturalistic or naturalistic terms is not a matter of concern. What *does* matter is each person's *personal experience* of "something more than self." And it is this *common core of experience* which, regardless of concepts or metaphors used, provides the basis for meaningful communication.

It is the personal experience of inner change which leads to an awareness of something greater when that has been lacking:

When I came into the program, I'd say I was spiritually bankrupt, and I didn't have any faith in any higher powers. For the first 2 years in A.A., I had a terrible time getting any kind of concept of a Higher Power. At first, of course, A.A. was my Higher Power—A.A. the group, the people in A.A. But since then, I've been able to get a lot out of this and broaden my conception of the Higher Power. (34-M-4/0)

My first impression of the spiritual part of the program was that it was complete nonsense. At first, I didn't turn my will and life over to the care of God. I just used the "24 hours at a time" [approach to not drinking]. After a while, I started realizing that "something" was keeping me sober. After about 6 months in the program, I came to realize that it is not "me" that keeps my heart beating, not "me" that keeps my brain functioning. There has to be some other power than "I" to keep my body alive. (34-M-1/0)

A change in thinking came about in similar fashion in the case of a friend who was an adamant atheist. When he was finally convinced that he simply could not control his drinking, or stop by himself, he entered a treatment center and then joined an A.A. group composed mostly of fellow professional men and women. A half year or more later, he and I were talking and he told me that his change in thinking about Power greater than himself started with the realization that some remarkable changes were going on inside him—changes that *he* certainly could not take credit for. And with reference to his well-known past disbeliefs, he smilingly admitted, "Even when the word 'God' is used by someone in the group, it doesn't bother me anymore."

We also note that when persons come to A.A. with negative, life-constricting concepts of God, their personal experience of inner change gives them a basis for revising their thinking about God:

In my case, I couldn't grasp the spirituality of the program. It was my concept of religion—my concept of God—a damning, hell-fire and brimstone type of thing—that blocked my understanding. In the beginning, I had to substitute the word "group" for the word "God." I can't say that there was any great awakening of lights turning on. It was just a gradual growing within of a sense of God. (36-M-0/9)

I had never lost faith in a Higher Power, but I was pleased with the spiritual part of the program because it changed my thinking about God—from a revengeful God to a loving God. (64-F-28/7)

I was really impressed with the spiritual part of the A.A. program. You see, I was afraid of God, but these people talked like God is their friend. He was with them all the time, and they didn't have their old worries and concerns. I was highly impressed that people could think of God as a good, close friend, or father. (46-F-9/2)

"Higher Power" is the term most often used among A.A. members when they talk about the "something greater" in their lives. To most, it is a new term, relatively free of unappealing connotations which "God" has for many. Also, many find that they can relate Higher Power more easily to their own growing experience of something greater operating in their lives. To illustrate:

I always did believe in God, although I am not much of a church-goer. But the idea of just the "Higher Power" and not naming God "God," I could accept that more easily. (48-F-8/3)

There are many who were helped by the use of "Higher Power" to rethink and clarify the whole "spiritual" area of the program:

> I think the spiritual part of the program is all wrapped up in the use of the words "Higher Power." This helped me to rethink my image of God. The terminology of these two words, "Higher Power," just did it for me—made it all snap into place. (55-F-14/6)

But others are in the stage of a thoughtful A.A woman in one of my classes who said, "My Higher Power is very real to me, and I now have a very real working relationship with my Higher Power. But for the life of me, I still can't reconcile it with a concept of God." Being an intellectually inclined person, she may by now have developed some concept which is compatible with her Higher-Power experience. But there are others in A.A. who never work this through intellectually, and still more who simply settle for using the word "God" synonymously with "Higher Power." But regardless of individual solutions to the conceptual problem, the common point of reference is the *inner experience* of life-giving power or Power.

Earlier, Tiebout was quoted as saying that unless the surrender of egocentric control occurred (whether suddenly or gradually) *and was also retained*, the "chances of remaining sober were minimal."

Or to put it in the language used at the beginning of this chapter: Unless an *inner shift in basic orientation to life* comes about *and is sustained*, enduring freedom from the obsession to drink is not likely to be achieved. And I described this basic shift in orientation as fundamentally an inner shift in "basic trust"—a shift from a trusting relationship with alcohol (and trust in the egocentric self in which alcohol has become central) toward a trusting relationship with life.

Even though this shift may have distinct and even dramatic moments, this letting go and becoming able to trust life is a process of continuing growth. In A.A. experience, as in psychotherapy, such growth is a continuing process of "working through"—of working through to an increasing trust in the nondefensive, positive aspects of one's own being—working through to increasingly nondefensive, trusting relationships with others. Intimately involved in both is a growing awareness of, and trust in, the supportive and creative forces (however conceptualized) which are operating in one's life.

Actually, most psychotherapists make the above assumptions in their therapeutic work with patients. Most count on what Carl Rogers called "the latent, inner resources of the individual" (1961). Harry Stack Sullivan spoke of an "intrinsic tendency toward maintaining or achieving mental health" (1945). Karen Horney came to the view that the major goal of psychotherapy was "the retrieval of the patient's inner springs of spontaneity and creativity" (1950). In her view, the "springs" are not to be created; they are assumed to be a given part of each person's life endowment and are to be retrieved.

Regardless of what else the term "Higher Power" may connote to a given reader, or to a given A.A. member, I believe it is vital to our understanding of A.A. to recognize that the "Higher Power" concept does include such inner powers.

To understand A.A. and its language use, it is also necessary to recognize that A.A.'s generally use "spiritual" in a broad sense. When they speak of "spiritual growth" they include growth away from what Freud called the narcissistic self—growth away from self-centeredness—growth in the direction of the new orientation we have been talking about.

One A.A. member, with almost 7 years in A.A., brought out the broader meaning of spirituality in this way:

> To me, spirituality is a feeling of acceptance of myself, of loving the other human being, and accepting what goes on in my life. It is the spirit of giving, the spirit of living. (40-F6/7)

Another member made reference to spiritual growth as "rising above one's present level of thinking, of asking, and of being." This "rising above" she attributed to the entire A.A. program which she thought of as "totally a spiritual program."

One of the frequently read and insightful statements is the following by Bill W.:

When a man or woman has a spiritual awakening, the most important meaning of it is that he has now become able to do, feel, and believe that which he could not do before on his unaided strength and resources alone. He has been granted a gift which amounts to a new state of consciousness and being. He has been set on a path which tells him he is really going somewhere, that life is not a dead end, not something to be endured or mastered. In a very real sense he has been transformed, because he has laid hold of a source of strength which, in one way or another, he had hitherto denied himself. He finds himself in possession of a degree of honesty, tolerance, unselfishness, peace of mind, and a love of which he had thought himself quite incapable.

(*Twelve Steps and Twelve Traditions*, p. 110)

Among A.A.'s, as I have indicated, the inner source of strength may be conceptualized in a great variety of ways, in either both supernaturalistic or naturalistic terms. It may not even be given any name at all:

I was raised a Roman Catholic and, at 16, decided that I did not like the religion. I threw God away, along with religion. When I came into A.A. the first time, I just had no feeling for the spiritual and paid no attention to it. But this last time in, I not only recognized that there is something which distinguishes me from a tree but that it is something very special that I have to look after, and pay attention to, as I am learning to care for myself. I now get a feeling for myself which seems to come more by way of saying: O.K., I don't know what it is and I don't even want to bother to put a name to it, but there is something beyond me that I can call on for help. I don't have to do things alone anymore.

And, I no longer have to control everything. . . . I do whatever I have to do about any problem, but I now believe it's going to be O.K.—that I'll get through it all right if I don't try to take it over myself. And, that's a good feeling. It's like I'm not God any-more—like I don't have to be God. (28-F-0/7)

In A.A. only 7 months this time around, this woman had not yet found a satisfactory term to apply to her newly found source of strength. But she now knew what the others were talking about when they spoke of a Higher Power. Further-more, she describes beautifully the essence of her new orienta-tion to life: no longer alone, struggling to make her way in a hostile world—but now going along with life and finding it to be supportive and trustworthy—now able to say "Yes" to life.

She would also nod in agreement upon hearing another member talking to fellow A.A.'s, summing up his new orienta-tion:

Through A.A., I have learned for the first time what living is. And I like it. Through you, the fellowship of A.A., I've learned how to meet life on its own ground—not on mine. This I am learning more and more all the time, and I hope to continue learning for the rest of my life.

SEVEN
A Program of Action

"Learning to meet life on its own ground"—this is what A.A. is all about. This is the nature of the reorientation which brings freedom from the obsessive relationship with drinking— brings it along with the wider freedom to relate more satisfyingly to life.

We have outlined and illustrated the changes in thinking and feeling which occur in the process of becoming alcoholic— changes with regard to drinking, self, others, and life in general—all interrelated in what becomes an obsessive field of forces. The more keenly aware we are of the obsessive strength of this old learning, the better we can appreciate the need for an *exceptionally favorable environment* in which to begin learning, and to continue learning, a new outlook on all the major aspects of life.

We have already touched upon some of the favorable elements in this new learning environment, and will point up other significant social aspects in the next chapter. However, the A.A. program is also, as its members say, "a program of *action*." Furthermore, the individual is provided with clear-cut *guides* for actions to take. These guides are not forced on the member. In fact, the person is told that he is free to work the program in his own way. Nevertheless, the guides for action are there.

The initial guidance given the newcomer stresses the importance of attending meetings. It is soon learned that this means lots of meetings—as many as possible. When groups abound, it may be suggested that the newcomer attend the meetings of a variety of groups and then select the group to which he feels most attracted and make that his "home group." It is also suggested that he start right in taking part in that group's activities, beginning with such simple things as emptying ash trays and putting chairs away.

The newcomer soon learns about alcoholism—that not taking the *first* drink is the logical emphasis and that this basic goal is best pursued just *one day at a time*.

All these bits of initial guidance are derived from the experiences of others—communicated by the first person or persons who call, by speakers who tell their stories in open meetings, and by other members in the informal talking before, after, or between meetings. Or it may be from the experiences of others via some of A.A.'s abundant literature.

Depending upon whom he talks to, the newcomer may be given other bits of initial guidance. However, he soon learns that the most basic suggestion of all is "to begin working the program." The "program" is often used in an inclusive sense to refer to everything about A.A., but here, the reference is to The Twelve Steps (found in full on pp. 90–91). These are action steps—presented as "the steps we took." These sum up the recovery process evolved by the early A.A.'s as they adapted what they had learned from their Oxford Group background and from their own experiences as recovering alcoholics.

We can see the major elements of the Twelve Steps more clearly in the set of Oxford Group idea which Bill's friend Ebby brought to him during his last hospitalization:

> You admit you are licked;
> you get honest with yourself;
> you talk it out with somebody else;
> you make restitution to the people you have harmed;
> you try to give of yourself without stint, with no demand for reward; and
> you pray to whatever God you think there is, even
> as an experiment. (*Alcoholics Anonymous Comes of Age*, pp. 62–63)

The Twelve Steps which finally evolved out of several years of personal recovery experiences and out of considerable trial-and-error experience in trying to reach other alcoholics and out of much discussion are as follows:

The Twelve Steps of Alcoholics Anonymous[1]

1. We admitted we were powerless over alcohol—that our lives had become unmanageable.
2. Came to believe that a Power greater than ourselves could restore us to sanity.
3. Made a decision to turn our will and our lives over to the care of God *as we understood Him.*
4. Made a searching and fearless moral inventory of ourselves.
5. Admitted to God, to ourselves, and to another human being the exact nature of our wrongs.

[1] *Alcoholics Anonymous* copyright © 1939, By Alcoholics Anonymous World Services, Inc. Reprinted by permission of A.A. World Services, Inc. Throughout this book, the opinions expressed in interpreting the Steps are those of the author. The interpretation accepted by A.A. appears in the books published by A.A. World Services, Inc.

6. Were entirely ready to have God remove all these defects of character.
7. Humbly asked Him to remove our shortcomings.
8. Made a list of all persons we had harmed, and became willing to make amends to them all.
9. Made direct amends to such people wherever possible, except when to do so would injure them or others.
10. Continued to take personal inventory and when we were wrong promptly admitted it.
11. Sought through prayer and meditation to improve our conscious contact with God *as we understood Him*, praying only for knowledge of His will for us and the power to carry that out.
12. Having had a spiritual awakening as the result of these steps, we tried to carry this message to alcoholics and to practice these principles in all our affairs.

The Twelve Steps are A.A.'s main road map. They are the central set of guides for action to be taken by the individual member. We have already discussed the important first three Steps and have illustrated how they were experienced by a spectrum of A.A. members. Here we look more closely at Steps Four through Twelve, remembering that all of the Twelve Steps are interrelated and mutually supportive; remembering also that "taking the Steps" and following other guides occur in a supportive social context. We shall also learn how a variety of A.A. members "worked the Steps"—each in his or her own way.

Even a quick reading of Steps Four through Twelve will point up their relevance to bringing about the basic changes in the alcoholic's world which we have been talking about.

In almost all psychotherapies, there is consensus about the importance of becoming honest with ourselves—of recognizing and dealing with our defensive distortions in outlook. There is consensus, as well, about the value of a cathartic unburdening of our guilts and hostilities, of our anxieties and fears—and doing so with another person who is understanding, nonjudgmental, and accepting. There is also consensus on the desirability of repairing damaged interpersonal relationships wherever feasible.

We note that the Steps recognize the need for "inner work" as well as interpersonal action. Becoming willing is often the difficult part, but action with other persons is the necessary follow-through.

There is also recognition of the long-term nature of the personal growth process—in Steps Ten and Eleven. And in Step Twelve, we have reference to the new orientation and its expression in action. In mutual-help groups, gathered to deal with a common problem, a two-way involvement with other group members is characteristic: *helping* and *being helped*. In A.A., it is a common observation that helping is the key to being helped. As A.A.'s say, "To keep it, you've got to give it away." And in an A.A. group, this means helping fellow members—or prospective fellow members.

Moreover, it is important to note that living by the new orientation is not to be confined to the world of A.A., but is to be extended to all of one's affairs—to all facets of one's life.

In addition to the Steps, there are other guides for action which have come into fellowship-wide use—and which rather quickly come to a newcomer's attention.

One is the so-called Serenity Prayer (correctly attributed to Reinhold Niebuhr, but having older roots) which reads: "God grant me the serenity to accept the things I cannot change, the courage to change the things I can, and the wisdom to know the difference." It came into use because the early A.A.'s found its distinctions to be particularly helpful in dealing not only with their powerlessness over alcohol but also with a great variety of problems and life situations. It is often used to open meetings, but its main use is as a personal guide.

One category of action guides consists of slogans and

aphorisms. These are easy to remember and they apply to a variety of common problem areas: ONE DAY AT A TIME— EASY DOES IT—FIRST THINGS FIRST are among the oldest and most-used slogans, along with LIVE AND LET LIVE, and THINK.

Already mentioned, particularly as counsel to newcomers, are "Don't compare—identify" and "Don't analyze—utilize." "Keep an open mind" is another. These and other guides are often referred to as *tools*—useful and handy:

> I used every tool they had. I was told to *stick with the winners* and I did; *go to meetings*, and I did. *Keep your memory green* was very important to me: to keep recalling what it felt like, the terrible remorse in the morning, the feelings of fear (of what, I wasn't sure), the feelings of sickness, a great deal of nausea. Another tool I used was *live and let live*, because I was a great one to stick my nose in somebody else's business and get all upset, carry a resentment, and start drinking. So I tried to learn to live and let live. (47-M-8/10)

The slogans and similar catch phrases may strike the reader as too simple—as downright "corny." Newcomers to A.A. often react the same way. But after a while, the same persons can laugh and say, "You know that you are making progress in the A.A. program when these corny slogans become gems of wisdom."

Being aware of A.A.'s major tools is one thing. However, we can learn much more about the A.A. recovery process by noting how the tools are used—particularly the varied ways in which this array of tools is drawn upon by individual members. First, let us see which tools members found to be most helpful at the beginning of their A.A. lives. Here is a range of responses to the interview question: At first, and during the first year or so of sobriety, what were the main A.A. tools you used to secure your sobriety?

The important first tool, for me, was the Serenity Prayer. I used that in just about everything I did. The slogans also. I really wasn't able to grasp anything more than the slogans and the Serenity Prayer. They were pretty basic—and they still are. (28-M-0/5)

The slogans and the Steps and the Serenity Prayer are the tools that I have used to obtain my sobriety so far. The meetings also, of course—seven to eight a week. (32-F-0/6)

I think my first tool was the fact that I cannot drink, and I used the Serenity Prayer to keep reminding me of that. (54-M-12/0)

I made use of the word "Think." At that time, the Serenity Prayer was still not of much use to me. But anytime I thought about a drink, I "thought the drink through" (to its full consequences) and that carried me through such times without drinking. (48-M-13/6)

One of the most basic aspects of the alcoholic's new orientation—the A.A. way of life—is the *realistic time perspective* of living in the present, taking things "one day at a time." Learning to do this is valuable in reaching a multitude of goals, but the first application is usually to the goal of not drinking:

Not taking that first drink seemed to me to be the most easily understandable idea. I knew and believed that there was no such thing as just one drink, for me. So, by taking it one day at a time and building those one-day-at-a-times like separate blocks, I got stronger as the weeks and months went by and was able to grasp other fundamentals in the program. (41-M-1/2)

I would say that my main tools, at first, and perhaps the only ones really, were this business of taking things a day at a time, and staying away from that first drink, one day at a time.[2] (68-M-13/0)

[2] Earlier movements, such as that of the Washingtonians, had all required a lifetime pledge of abstinence. To an alcoholic, this is a very forbidding prospect; but not taking a drink, just today, is conceivable to most.

Further perspective is provided in additional responses to the query about the tools used at first:

Fellowship, telephone numbers. But of all the tools, the Serenity Prayer was perhaps the greatest single thing that has ever affected my life. Also attendance at meetings—the ability to listen to other people and absorb from them. (68-M-10/8)

It was "Easy does it" and "One day at a time." Meetings every night, helping make the coffee, picking up the ashtrays, putting back chairs, and *listening* [his emphasis]. (37-M-0/9)

I used the slogans, the sayings and the Fourth and Fifth Steps [inventory and catharsis]—plus a dialogue with my sponsor. (25-M-0/8)

The first thing I latched onto when I came into the program was the slogans. They were visible [displayed] in the meetings and "Easy does it" and "First things first" really stood out for me. I find I still apply them; they helped me a lot. Now, I try to be involved in all aspects of A.A.—working the program as it is suggested—the Steps, the Serenity Prayer, the spiritual side, the meetings. (32-M-0/7)

The last statement represents the ideal pattern: "to be involved in all aspects of A.A." and "working the program as it is suggested." But individual members begin where they can and move forward as they are able—and they are given the freedom to do so.

At first, some rely heavily on one or more persons:

The main tools I used at first were the telephone and relying on other people to get me through very frightening episodes. I used the a-day-at-a-time idea and eventually the whole concept of turning over what I could not do anything about to "something." I wouldn't say it was a Higher Power because I still rejected that. (32-F-0/6)

One tool I had to use was a sponsor. That had to do until I could work out, in my own thinking, an approach to contact with a Higher Power. From my sponsor I learned: one day at a time, keeping things simple, not analyzing, attending meetings, and accepting the fact that I had an illness. She advised me to take care of my health, get enough sleep, eat properly, keep regular hours. It is a rather jolting transition because as an active alcoholic you don't do any of these things. So, all these very good common-sense things are repeated to you, time and again in A.A., until you finally do them automatically. (50-F-13/5)

In the following two accounts we have further descriptions of the varied ways in which individuals make use of A.A. tools, including the Steps:

In addition to the Serenity Prayer, which I used heavily in the beginning, I recall latching on to "Easy does it" and applying it in all areas of my life. I realized that I was a very hyper type of person and needed to slow down. That led to other slogans. I attended meetings every night. I did a lot of writing down of my feelings—a lot of inventory writing [Fourth Step]. I used a lot of other tools, right from the beginning. I would say that my main tools [after 15 months in A.A.] are going to two "Step meetings" a week for study and discussion of the Steps, and making a conscious effort to apply the Twelve Steps to all my affairs. (44-M-1/3)

I think the only conscious effort I made at first was to attend many meetings and to listen with an open mind and not prejudge or be critical. I am not an open-minded person. I have tended to shun advice; and when others have made suggestions, I would do the opposite or as near opposite as I could manage. So it seems like a God-given thing that I was able to keep a fairly open mind when I came to A.A.

And, I've gotten into the Steps. In the course of these three years, I have worked the first eight. But each time I've worked another Step, it's been a kind of push-come-to-shove thing. I would wait until I felt uncomfortable and realized that the reason was that I wasn't growing—nothing was happening—and I took that as an indication that I should go on to the next step in the program. Taking these Steps has been a great help to me. So, through the Steps, the meetings, and the fellowship, I am developing a spiritual side to my life, something I never had before. My wife is also in Al-Anon, and we are working together in trying to build a life as a couple. This has also helped. (38-M-3/2)

Despite the centrality of the Twelve Steps in A.A., there are some members who do not get around to taking them seriously for a long time. In the following report, we have a man who thought of himself as an A.A. member for about 9 years, attending two or three times a week, achieving periods of abstinence of varying lengths, but never thinking of the Twelve Steps as requiring much action on his part. After all, as he said, he already believed in God and hadn't committed any crimes:

For 9 years after coming to my first A.A. meeting, I would have periods of dryness of varying lengths, but I would always go back to nibbling and eventually to a drunk. Toward the end of that time, after an 11-month period of dryness, I started nibbling again. Instead of a month or so, this time I was back in a drying-out place within 2 weeks. And, about 2 months later, I was back in the drying-out place after only 4 days of drinking. Coming out of this last one, the progression [progressive nature of the illness] really hit me, and I knew that I had better stop playing around with this thing and really do something about it. I also realized that in the 9 years, other people in A.A. were staying sober, but I wasn't. Obviously, I must be missing something.

So, I determined to find out what it was, and start from scratch with Step One. I believe that, during the 9 years, I had never really taken that Step—had never really accepted my powerlessness over alcohol. I always had the reservation that somehow, someday, I was going to be able to beat it. Now convinced of my powerlessness over alcohol, I went through all the Steps thoroughly and with some purpose. I also began working with others and helping others. Now [almost 2½ years sober] I keep going to meetings an average of five nights a week. I work with others, and I'm continually in contact with others in A.A. every day. I also join in the group activities. (62-M-2/5)

A very important activity, in A.A. parlance, is "Twelfth Step work." This refers to "carrying this message to alcoholics." Broadly, Twelfth Step work refers not only to helping prospects get started in A.A., but includes all action in helping another alcoholic in his recovery, including the longer-time role of sponsorship. A Twelfth Step *call*, however, refers specifically to calling on an alcoholic who has asked for help. The "Twelfth Stepper" may or may not become the new person's sponsor, but usually does serve as a temporary sponsor.

The value of a personal Twelfth Step call on the alcoholic who has requested help needs no comment. Less obvious, however, are the several important functions which such a call may have on the Twelfth Step caller himself.

"Keeping the memory green" is one of the major functions. If the A.A. member has begun to forget how it was, or has begun to idealize drinking, then making a Twelfth Step call on an alcoholic who is just coming off a binge is a vivid reminder. As the woman quoted in an earlier chapter stated, "It was like seeing a movie of myself." She could no longer gloss over what her own condition had once been. Now, for the first time, she said, the full reality hit home.

Another initial value to the Twelfth Step caller, is the discovery that certain deficits of his alcoholic past have now become assets. As Joan Jackson stated, "Even the aspects of his past of which he feels most ashamed prove to be useful tools for communicating with the guilt-ridden, hopeless alcoholic he is trying to reach. Thus, . . . his alcoholism becomes one of the bases upon which he can build new and rewarding relationships" (*A Second Look at A.A.*, unpublished paper).

A Twelfth Step call may also provide the caller with

perspective on his own progress. There may be times when, even though he is sober, he feels discouraged with himself: There may seem to be so little change—or no change at all. Calling on an active alcoholic provides a realistic yardstick—a corrective reminder—of how far he *has* come. The chances are that this experience will also renew his motivation to keep going forward.

Of course the Twelfth Step caller may not succeed in getting the alcoholic to go to A.A. It would be natural for the caller to be disappointed—or even to feel that he has personally failed. For this reason, A.A.'s are constantly reminded that, in such cases, the *main* value of the call has nevertheless been achieved, namely, the strengthening of the caller's own sobriety. What is meant by this is well illustrated in the following evaluation of the tools which this member used:

I would say the main thing that helped me get sober in the first place was the idea of staying sober just one day at a time. This is the big thing my sponsor told me—also, that I could work the program any way I wanted to. But I believe what kept me sober was my first experience with helping another guy get sober. That did something to me that I had never really had happened to me before—that I was able to help someone else without any personal gain whatsoever in mind. This was my main turning point in A.A. (58-M-20/0)

We can hardly exaggerate the recovery value of all Twelfth Step activity. It will be recalled that one of the six recovery principles which Ebby first brought to Bill was: "You try to give of yourself without stint, with no demand for reward." We have also cited Bill's early experience that when he genuinely tried to help another alcoholic (got involved, forgot himself) this helped him more than any other action to keep from drinking when the compulsion to drink was strong. So from the beginning of A.A., such helping activity has been held to be a very basic component of the helper's *own* recovery—of his *own* reorientation to life.

This continues to be the experience of A.A. members. Here is a man with over 4 years of sobriety in A.A. who stated:

The main tools that I use now to maintain my sobriety are: to be active in the A.A. group; to continue to practice the A.A. program; and to keep myself busy trying to assist another alcoholic with his problem. (43-M-4/4)

From an "old-timer," a man with over 24 years of sobriety, comes this perspective.

I've needed all the tools in A.A. But the three main ones would be: going to meetings, which I consider very essential; second, is taking the A.A. program seriously in every respect—that is, not merely talking the Twelve Steps but trying to live them and act them; and the third most important thing is this unselfish giving of oneself to help the other guy or gal obtain sobriety. (72-M-24-5)

As we note in these last three reports, Twelfth Step work becomes more than just one of A.A.'s many tools. It is basic. At first, it may serve as a counter to the compulsion to drink. But as alcoholics gradually emerge from their egocentric shells, the "unselfish giving of oneself" increasingly becomes a central aspect of their developing new orientation.

In the following interview segments, we have descriptions of tool-use from the perspective of 4 or more years in A.A.:

The first 9 months that I was on the program, I averaged 10 meetings a week—never less than five and as high as 13. The main tool I used was meetings. But I was also on the phone constantly; and I socialized almost exclusively with people on the program. It was all-consuming at first, but I had to have it—I think I fought it that hard. I didn't always feel comfortable at meetings, but I always felt secure at meetings. I was exposed to a lot of guys who were also willing to go to this many meetings, and this also helped. The first thing was sobriety, and everything else was secondary. Now, I average around four meetings a week. Sobriety is still the number one priority, but there are other things, and I'm trying to get some balance in my life. (33-M-3/4)

The next man, after a year in A.A. during which he thought he had accepted his alcoholism and the A.A. program, went on what he called "the worst drunk that I ever had." He came back to A.A. "feeling very hopeless and very frightened and very sick." This time, he was able to accept and openly acknowledge his powerlessness over alcohol. Looking back from the perspective of almost 10 years, he thought:

The thing that helped me the most, and provided the most dramatic break-through, was taking the Third Step [surrender decision] very early in this second go-around. I was really in a corner and seething with a lot of resentments. I knew that somehow or other I had to get rid of these resentments or I would go and get drunk again. That sort of forced me into taking the Third Step—and that really began to open things up for me. Also, in the meetings, even though I had heard so much of it before, I listened carefully to see what I had missed. I went to meetings practically every night of the week.

Now, I still go to three or four meetings a week, because I love to go, but I'm now trying to bring some balance into my life—giving A.A. a certain amount of time, and a certain amount to home and family. In A.A., I go out some on speaking commitments [speaking at meetings of other groups]. I involve myself to a certain extent in Twelfth Step work with newcomers—and with the Twelve Steps themselves. Another tool that is working for me is an effort toward self-acceptance, without the moralizing and judging which always seem to generate guilts and anxieties in me. Just trying to accept myself for what I am, and the way I am, is a big help. (37-M-9/11)

Sometimes, non-A.A.'s wonder why many members continue to be active in A.A. after they have not had a drink for 3 or 4 years. I believe the above man speaks for the majority of those who continue to go to meetings: "because I love to go."

Perhaps, by now, we can better understand why so many feel that way. The total A.A. environment provides *more* than freedom from the compulsion to drink. It helps its members to keep growing in their new orientation to life—growing in a way of life which they have found to be more productive and satisfying. In short, they like what is happening to them, and they want more of it. So they keep putting themselves in the social environment in which, somehow, the desirable changes are nourished.

Let us explore this "somehow" some more—trying to make explicit the social and interpersonal dynamics which are operating in the usual A.A. social environment.

EIGHT
Involvement with Others

Structurally, the basic social unit in Alcoholics Anonymous is the group—a local group—and each group holds one or more meetings a week.

It is at meetings that a new person really begins his involvement with other A.A. members—an involvement which, usually, will extend to becoming integrated into a specific group.

When groups are small, regular attendance at meetings rather easily leads to involvement in the group. Even today, in most localities, groups are on the small side—under 25 members. But in many urban and suburban areas where there are many meetings, with some speaker meetings having a hundred or even several hundred persons present, and where there is much visiting of each other's groups, it is possible for a person to attend many meetings without becoming involved in any group. Under these circumstances, the counsel to new members is not just to keep attending meetings, but to select a specific group and make that his or her "home group" by becoming involved with the others in the group.

That is what group membership means in A.A.: *Involvement.* Unlike membership in most organizations, membership in A.A. is self-determined. There are no screening committees. All groups are to be open to any alcoholic who wants help. This means that it is up to the individual to decide if he qualifies. As for "joining" a particular group, there again it is not the group but the individual who decides that he will be a member of a certain group. In effect, that decision is indicated by regular participation in that group and its activities. It is as simple as that.

Some groups will acknowledge the individual's intention and involvement by the formality of asking him to join the group— or by simply adding his name to the group roster. But most groups do not bother with even this minimum formality. Members of most groups are simply considered to be those who show up regularly, take part, and, in effect, say that this is their "home group."

Here are several reports illustrating the joining process:

In my mind, I "joined A.A." and "joined a group" the same night. I just went to that group's meetings and continued to go until someone took my name down, and I was a member. (27-M-2/6)

I don't know when I joined my group. Within 6 months of my going to A.A., this group was my main base. The people there were close to me everyday, and I more or less used the whole group as my sponsor for awhile. I could get to any one of them when I felt I needed to. (40-M-10/1)

I was 6 months in the program, maybe more, when I got asked to join a group, the group I'm in now. I don't know why it took me that long to join a group. I had been to the meetings of plenty of groups, and I liked the people in every group. I think in the back of my mind I had a reservation: If I joined a group, that was it. I would have to become part of that group, would have to be active, and I would definitely have to stay away from that first drink. (Female)

In the last sentence, the woman revealed her awareness that membership in a group would require more of her in terms of commitment and involvement. She recognized that it would mean both the setting aside of lingering reservations and a greater personal involvement in the group's life and a set of close relationships within the group.

That, of course, is what A.A. has to offer. Anything less than high involvement means only marginal participation— only a partial experience of A.A.'s full dynamics. This recognition is well expressed in the following:

I guess I joined a group about a year and a half after I first came to A.A. I did this [after some slipping] because I knew from what I was reading and from what I was being told at meetings and by listening to the experiences of others, *that you had to become really a part of A.A.* if it was going to work for you. At this point, I desperately wanted it to work for me—and I had become convinced that this meant *really being in a group.* (38-F-0/7)

Really being in a group, this is what it takes for A.A. to work at its best. This does not preclude attending the meetings of other groups in addition to one's own—or making close friends with A.A. members outside one's home group. With a good home base, these other contacts enrich rather than dilute one's A.A. experience. But a strong home-group life is important. This is something to be kept in mind by all who refer an alcoholic to A.A.—by all who work with a person trying to make it in A.A.

We speak of the person as selecting or choosing a home group. Actually, all kinds of factors may enter into such a choice. It may simply be location: "I went to the group which met nearest to where I live." It may simply be the first group one is introduced to. Or, it may be other factors which influence the choice such as those brought out in the following reports:

I joined a group about 3 months after going to A.A. I was attending the meetings of one group more than others, but it was 3 months before I settled on that one and considered it to be my group, my home group. I seemed to be able to identify better with the people in it. They were people who were more prone to help, to be more supportive, and I thought they set good examples. (57-M-12/2)

I was on the A.A. program about 6 months before I joined a group. It was a new group and a small group, and I liked that. It was a "Big Book" group (focusing on the study and discussion of the basic text, *Alcoholics Anonymous*) and it was close to where I lived at the time, and also met on the night of the week I wanted. (42-F-2/6)

The reason I joined this particular group was the fact that I found a larger group to be too impersonal. This smaller group was much more intimate in terms of continuity of contact with specific individuals. (57-M-0/2)

The following two interview segments are of particular interest because they refer to the very same group—a young people's group. They reveal different aspects of the same group, but also illustrate the fact that the attractiveness of a group is in part a function of what the individual perceives and feels he needs at the time:

I joined this group because it was a group of younger people of my age bracket who were experiencing the same problems that I was having. Other groups had a lot of older people who didn't have children growing up and weren't young guys starting out in business or early in their careers. The peer group was a lot easier to get along with. The fellows seemed to understand more. Most everyone had a little higher education, and we are able to communicate with each other. Our goals and aspirations are all pretty much the same. (36-M-6/9)

The second man, returning to A.A. after a bad time:

I was truly desperate. I attended several different meetings, and I was searching for a group that I could really fit in with. When I got to the Young People's Group, I saw what appeared to me—and later turned out to be correct—to be a very active, intense group as far as the program was concerned. Everyone seemed to care about it. It was a discussion group, and they really hammered out what A.A. is. I just had a vague knowledge until then. They spoke constantly of the Steps. I said, "This is for me. I know I have to change my life and this is what it takes." (39-M-?)

In the course of time, a member may change to another group. This may occur because of a change in residence. Or it may come about as a result of visiting the meetings of other groups. In the other meetings, one may strike up new friendships which are particularly meaningful—or one may like the flavor or some feature of a particular meeting and find himself becoming more involved with members of this group. A person may think of this new involvement as simply added to his continued participation in his own home group, or he may eventually consider the new group to be his home group.

A more common shift is not from one group to another, but a change in type of meeting preferred: from *speaker* meetings to *discussion* meetings. Because most groups hold both types of meetings, this change in preference usually does not mean a change of groups. Newcomers are generally taken to speaker meetings because experience had shown that the immediate needs of a new person are usually better met there. But, sooner or later, the new person will likely be attending discussion meetings as well, and eventually, will probably find himself preferring them.

At first, I think I received my biggest benefit from listening to the stories in the open speaker meetings. There, I could kind of put it all together and see the kind of person I was—and what booze was doing to me. Then, I was able to open up and give a little of myself at a small, closed discussion meeting. (50-M-3/0)

In the first 3 or 4 months, I preferred open speaker meetings because it was easier. All I had to do was sit—and that's about all I was capable of doing. Then I began going to closed meetings also—and I started to like these a little better because we broke down into smaller groups and were able to start talking about our defects and problems. Today [after almost 7 years], when I want to do work, I go to closed meetings. When I want to socialize, it's open meetings. (54-M-6/7)

I liked both speaker and discussion meetings equally well in the beginning. I needed the identification (with speakers). But I also needed thought from everyone. Now, I much prefer a closed Step meeting because I'm at a point in my program where I need the gut-level A.A. (42-F-3/7)

Despite this common shift in meeting preference, almost all A.A.'s continue to find value in both speaker and discussion meetings:

In the beginning, I mainly went to open speaker meetings. But to maintain my sobriety, I feel it is important for me to go to both open and closed meetings. In open meetings, I find there is a lot of identification that I have to keep using. In closed meetings, especially Step meetings, we talk about the Steps, and I feel that this is very important in my life—for if I don't keep the Steps in front of me, it is very easy to forget to use them. (34-M-4/10)

In the beginning, I preferred the open meetings. I now attend a variety of meetings—open speaker, closed discussion, and Step meetings. I believe I get something out of each. One type of meeting does not seem to be enough. I need the full coverage. (62-M-2/5)

Of the two major types of A.A. meetings, there is a greater amount of interpersonal interaction in the discussion meetings.

Yet even at their best, discussion meetings are not the settings for the most intimate and potent social dynamics. As was indicated in the opening chapter, it is outside the formal meetings that the greatest amount of interaction as well as the most uninhibited and dynamic interaction takes place. Meetings are visible and very important. Without them there would be no A.A. But, we cannot appreciate A.A.'s total social dynamics until we also become fully aware of the *quantity* and *quality* of the interpersonal interaction which takes place *before*, *after*, and particularly *between* meetings. Most A.A. members spend many more hours in such interaction than in meetings.

Most of the before, after, and between meeting hours are naturally spent talking on a one-to-one basis—or in small clusters—with certain members of one's own group, persons with whom one develops an especially close relationship. But as a result of attending the meetings of other groups, or having others attend one's own group, additional close relationships frequently develop. We are given a better picture of this little-seen part of A.A. interaction in the following sample of replies to the interview questions: With how many A.A.'s in your own group do you have a close relationship? With how many outside your group?

I consider all of the A.A.'s in my group to be my friends and a part of me. There are a few, primarily women, that I share my life with more than I do with others, but I can't put it in exact numbers, perhaps a half dozen or so. And, I have a very close personal relationship with about the same number of A.A.'s outside my group. (50-F-1/4)

In the group I am a member of—about 12 of us in the group—there are two that I would say are close friends. The kind of closeness that I have with these two is such that I would tell them anything in the world, no holds barred. Outside the group, there are three that I have a real closeness to. (44-F-18/10)

I find one man's response to the question very revealing— telling us something about the quality of A.A. relationships in general:

It is very difficult to say how many "close" relationships I have within my own group because I consider the relationships with *all* members to be much closer than I was used to having with *any* human being before I got into A.A. I am closer to some than to others, but there are a great many. (39-M-0/7)

A relationship with a *sponsor* is often the first close relationship for a new person in A.A. In the following, we have what A.A.'s would consider to be an ideal sponsorship relationship:

I felt free to seek advice from my sponsor. I was going to meetings, and he would meet me there as often as he could, approximately three times a week. For the first 2 months, I was also in touch with him on the phone every day, sometimes twice a day. After meetings, we would sometimes talk for 2 hours or so and just get everything straightened out, so to speak. (36-M-0/9)

A good sponsorship relationship generates a closeness which is likely to continue after the initial period of very frequent contact. The following is an example of such continuing contact in the case of a woman who was herself a very active sponsor:

I am in close contact with a lot of people because I did sponsor an awful lot of girls. Even the girls that by now have five years of sobriety, or something like that, are still in close contact with me. I couldn't give you a number. My phone rings constantly, and I am in frequent personal contact. I am in contact with many, many people—people that I help, and also people whose help I need. (40-F-6/11)

"Taking the Fifth Step," (admitting "to another human being the exact nature of our wrongs") if it is taken with another A.A. member, is another intimate occasion which leads to an extra degree of closeness:

> In my group, I have a very close relationship with about a half dozen. Maybe seven or eight outside of my group. Now, when I say "close relationship," these are people that I have taken the Fifth Step with, and they with me. That means pretty close! (57-M-12/2)

We now have a more complete and realistic picture of the actual A.A. social environment than is normally connoted by words like "groups" and "meetings." It is my view that of all the social dynamics in A.A. the ones with the greatest leverage for personal change are to be found in the warm, honest, intimate interaction within close, interpersonal relationships.

We also see that each A.A. member will develop his own unique constellation of such close relationships—his own particular set of significant others—drawn from within his home group and often from outside his home group as well. How large the constellation can become in some cases is shown in the following:

> Within my present group, there are three or four people that I manage to speak to between meetings, three or four times a week. There are at least 10 in the group that I would have no hesitation in calling up if I ran into a difficult moment in the day. That's in the group I belong to. Outside my group—and I attend meetings in a number of locations—I feel like I've gained a world of friends. I should imagine that there are around 30 that I could call up and get into a meaningful conversation in terms of both helping them, and getting help for myself, should the occasion arise. (41-M-1/2)

> I feel close to all of the people in my group, but, off hand, I would say that I have a very close relationship with perhaps a dozen. As for A.A. members outside of my own group, well, I would say that, in my phone book, there must be 50 or 60 names of members I would not hesitate to call. (42-F-3/9)

In the first chapter, I referred to Yalom's analysis (1975) of the "core" therapeutic factors which he found to be the chief change-producing factors common to the various group psychotherapies, regardless of their distinctive "fronts" of language, concepts, practices, etc. Reading Yalom, I was fascinated with the application of his analysis and findings to A.A.

A.A.'s front of language, concepts, and practices is indeed quite different from that of any of the standard psychotherapies. But when we look at the change-producing core factors, we cannot but be impressed by the extent to which they are present and operative in the A.A. social environment.

From what has been presented so far, we can quickly recognize three of Yalom's basic change factors: *instilling of hope, universality* (learning that one's alcoholism and related problems are not unique), and the *imparting of information* regarding both the nature of the problem and the path to recovery. Furthermore, A.A.'s basic method of honest and open sharing of one's personal experience is an exceptionally effective way of achieving these ends. In the self-revealing stories, we have the power of real-life drama. There is an intimate entering into the struggles and despairs of other human beings caught in the same powerlessness. One no longer feels so guilty alone:

> In the speaker meetings, I could identify with just about every speaker with regard to some aspect of his or her story, and it made me feel that I wasn't alone. My life wasn't the only good-for-nothing existence that there ever was. (32-M-0/8)

Through the stories of others, a new person also gains new information about alcoholism—what it *is* as well as what it *is not*. And as members tell about their recovery experiences, not only is hope instilled, but a person also begins to learn about the basic elements of the A.A. recovery process.

Catharsis is another change factor Yalom listed which plays a very large role in A.A. dynamics. We see one level of it in the telling of one's own story in speaker meetings. It is true that these stories center around the problem of alcoholism, which some critics feel is too narrow a focus. But as I have tried to show, alcoholism is anything but a narrow matter. It involves important changes throughout each person's total field. Moreover, sobriety, as A.A.'s use the term, means changes in oneself far beyond not drinking.

The model for telling one's story in speaker meetings is telling what it was like, what happened, and what it is like now. Some speakers are not yet comfortable with more than telling what it was like—what A.A.'s call drunk-a-logs or blow-by-blow bottle stories. But others tell their stories in a very insightful and revealing way, including their recovery stories.

It is the A.A. norm that stories are to be told without notes, with the result that speakers are sometimes surprised at what comes out: forgotten material recalled or new, self-revealing insights—products of free association. Additional catharsis takes place in discussion meetings—more so, of course, in some groups than in others. But as we have emphasized, the most open and hair-down interaction takes place outside of meetings. That is where the greatest amount and the greatest depth of catharsis takes place—with one's sponsor or with select others with whom one feels free to open up.

As for catharsis of repressed hostility, it is true that it is not A.A. practice to use the expression of anger toward another group member as a therapeutic tool as is done in some types of professionally guided group sessions. But this does not mean that hostility and anger remain repressed and not dealt with. On the contrary, *resentments*, the A.A. term for unresolved hostile and angry feelings, are treated in A.A. literature as "enemy number one," freedom from which is considered to be of prime importance.

Where then does the catharsis of these hostile, angry feelings take place? Occasionally, even in speaker meetings. I have heard persons when telling their stories unload considerable feeling about some "big, fat resentment." More often, such ventilating occurs in the smaller discussion meetings. Still more often, resentments can be aired with one's sponsor or some other member with whom one feels free to open up. Finally, for angers not so expressed, there is the Fifth Step expectation of a more thorough catharsis with another human being—a person who may be a fellow member or may be a professional person.

But, it should also be noted that a good deal of repressed anger and hostility (not all) gets dissipated with the surrender process discussed in Chapter 6. Furthermore, with a friendlier view of oneself, other people, and the world, less anger is generated—one simply perceives less to be angry about.

Yalom identifies seven other dynamic factors found in the various group psychotherapies.[1] However, only a reading of Yalom's insightful and thorough discussion of these "curative factors" can convey the full dynamic reality of each of them—and thus sharpen the reader's perception of their functioning not only in group psychotherapy but also somewhere in the total A.A. social environment.

Furthermore, we may note that the dynamic quality of these therapeutic factors in A.A. is enhanced by the attitudes and personal qualities which A.A.'s typically exhibit toward each other. These enhancing qualities are the very same personal qualities which have been found to be characteristic of professional helpers who are exceptionally helpful.

In the language of Carl Rogers (1961) such effective helpers relate to the persons they help with *unconditional positive regard* (warm acceptance); with *genuineness and transparency*, i.e., with *openness, being one's real being*; and with *empathy* ("a sensitive ability to see the other person and his

---

[1] Corrective recapitulation of primary family life, interpersonal learning, imitative behavior (modeling), development of socializing techniques, group cohesiveness, altruism, and existential factors. (Yalom, 1975, pp. 3–104)

world as the other person sees them"—plus the ability to communicate accurately what he sees).

We saw in Chapter 4, how much newcomers to A.A. were impressed by these very qualities. We repeat certain statements:

These people understood what I've been through.
These people knew what they were talking about. They had all gone through the mill that I had.
I remember the truthfulness and honesty of all.
I felt these were people who cared.
I found warmth, I found love, and I found acceptance.
I just could not believe the level of acceptance I saw there. I had never seen such accepting people in my life—accepting not just of me but of each other. There were very warm feelings—in a way like coming home.

In these typical reactions, we note not only understanding and empathy, but also an exceptional effectiveness in communicating that understanding. We also note an unusual degree of honesty and nondefensive openness. And we have a strikingly high level of acceptance. In these qualities, we have a major key to A.A.'s effectiveness in reaching the alcoholic to begin with; in helping him to face, admit, and accept his powerlessness over alcohol; and also in bringing about the basic changes in behavior and orientation to life which the A.A. program calls for.

We may say several things about these qualities. They are qualities which make for the ease of communication which is so noticeable in A.A. and is associated with the family feeling and group cohesiveness. They are qualities which help the individual to be drawn out of the egocentric shell, become interested in others, and accept them as they are. They are qualities which help to release untapped inner resources and to change the person's view of life and the meaning of his or her own existence.

NINE
More Than Sobriety

We are now in a position to round out our perspective on the recovery process in Alcoholics Anonymous. In the previous chapter, I pointed out some of the psychotherapeutic factors present in A.A. which, despite the lay language, are clearly recognizable. Not only that, but in many respects, these dynamic factors are operating with unusual effectiveness.

In A.A., as in psychotherapy, the goal is a "working through" to an increasingly nondefensive, productive relationship with oneself, with other persons, and with life. Furthermore, both A.A. and psychotherapy (whether in a group or on a one-to-one basis) rely heavily on interpersonal interaction for the working through. In so many ways, A.A. makes sense from a psychotherapeutic perspective.

However, I hold that we have a more complete view of A.A. if we *also* look upon it as a *society* and a *culture*; and if we also perceive the A.A. experience to be a resocializing or accultur-

ating process—the joining of a new society and being socialized into its culture, its way of life.

In previous chapters, we have looked at the guides for action
and many characteristics of the A.A. social environment.
Viewing A.A. as a society and culture will bring out several
aspects worthy of our attention.

In Chapter 4, we spoke of coming into A.A. as "entering a
new society." Of course, A.A. is a sub-society within the
larger society, but it is nevertheless a distinct society. Even so,
A.A. is basically a *transitional society* in the sense that a major
goal is to restore the alcoholic to the status of a well-
functioning member of the larger society, satisfactorily fulfilling his various social roles. A.A. can be valued for this
function alone.

A major reason, however, why A.A. is successful as a
transitional society is the fact that it is a *specialized society*. It
is attuned to the special feelings and outlook of persons who
have become alcoholic. To a professional psychotherapist
dealing with individuals, the internal dynamics of the various
dependencies (alcohol, other drugs, gambling, etc.) may appear to be much the same. Nevertheless, their respective
social worlds are not at all alike. Each has its own language,
norms, and subleties of past experiences. Each has its own
universe of discourse. Alcoholics have individual differences,
but they have so much experience in common that they are
able to communicate more easily and fully with each other—
and able to identify with each other in a deeply felt manner.
The value of this high degree of identification with each other
should never be underestimated.

We should also note that A.A. is a very *cohesive society*, in
large part because of its specialization. Yalom (pp. 45–69)
notes that the quality of a group's cohesiveness is an important
variable in the effectiveness of group psychotherapy.

The same point was brought out by an observant A.A.
friend. In a conversation, he had characterized two neighbor-

ing A.A. groups as "good groups." I asked him what made them good. Without hesitation he replied:

Because they hang together. When they have somebody new they all work with him. It is not just a one-sponsor deal; everyone works with him. And, the atmosphere in these groups makes you feel at home. In some groups, you don't have this homey atmosphere, and you don't have everybody working together.

Local groups *do* vary in the degree of cohesiveness—as indeed they do with respect to any group quality. We may also note that, over time, the same group may fluctuate in its cohesiveness. Nevertheless, overall, by any comparative measure, A.A. groups, singly and collectively, constitute an exceptionally cohesive society.

Like all societies, A.A. also has a *culture*. A society's culture includes all normative or customary ways of thinking, feeling, and behaving. Central to such normative ways are (1) the ideas and "facts" which are accepted as true, (2) the values believed in, and (3) the standard ways of perceiving oneself and others in a social field (Lewin 1951).

We have seen that becoming alcoholic involves changes in all of these respects—in ideas, "facts," values, and perceptions of self, others, and life in general.

In turn, A.A. may be viewed as a society having a culture which consists of a corrective set of normative ideas, facts, values, and perceptions of self, others and life.

Among themselves, A.A.'s do not use the terminology of the social scientist, but they have their own way of referring to their culture, the most common being "the A.A. way of life" or, sometimes, "the program." They recognize that close association and involvement with other members in the A.A. society are necessary for learning the A.A. way of life. Furthermore, there even seems to be a recognition that society and culture are simply two aspects of the same totality, reflected in their dual use of the designation "A.A." to refer to both the way of life and the society.

Some years ago, Kurt Lewin and Paul Grabbe (1949) observed that acceptance of a new group's culture is intimately tied to the acceptance of belongingness in the new group itself. They hypothesized that the acceptance of the group is usually prerequisite to the acceptance of that group's ideas, values, perceptions, etc. Since then, my observations have led me to concur. In "buying" the A.A. program—the new culture—the majority of A.A.'s are first sold on the people in A.A., and almost all are highly influenced in their acceptance of the A.A. program by their favorable impression of the people in A.A. One of A.A.'s great strengths lies in the appealing qualities of empathic understanding, concern, and unconditional acceptance which the new person is shown by the people in A.A., so well illustrated in Chapter 4.

In such a warm, understanding environment, it is much easier to be open to the group-shared ways of thinking and doing—and to begin incorporating them as one's own.

As stated in Chapter 5, one of the most difficult ideas or facts for the alcoholic to accept is the reality of his powerlessness over alcohol. Equally difficult to accept is the unbelievable further reality that life can be satisfying—even more satisfying—without alcohol, and the reality that there are life forces which can be trusted to bring release from the compulsive relationship to drinking, and can be trusted to support the new alcohol-free orientation to life.

Considering the enormity of such a change in beliefs and behavior, it is only logical that the prime focus in open speaker meetings should be upon helping newcomers face these radically different "truths" and thus get started on the A.A. path to sobriety.

We have noted before that in A.A., sobriety comes to mean much more than not drinking. However, not drinking is necessarily the first focus of attention for the new person in A.A. Because controlling the extent of drinking, once started, is no longer possible, the attention is focused on "not taking the first drink." To put this new goal within reach, the time frame is to be just one day at a time: not drinking today.

Of course, the new person is also urged to keep coming to meetings—a simple way of saying, "Keep exposing yourself to the A.A. people and the A.A. program." A.A.'s do not generally go beyond such formulations, but from my social science point of view, they are nevertheless recognizing the importance of the A.A. social environment which provides not only understanding, concern, and social support, but constitutes *a society* which is both the *carrier of*, and the *medium for learning*. A.A.'s way of life—A.A.'s *culture*.

Non-A.A. observers who attend only open speaker meetings can easily obtain an incomplete and even distorted view of A.A. because of the rather heavy emphasis upon the not-drinking meaning of sobriety. Speaker meetings, as we saw, have something of value for persons at each stage of their resocialization, but the stories told by speakers are often, at least in part, directed to the persons new on the program and to those not yet comfortably secure in their sobriety.

However, as a person moves along in A.A., more and more of his attention will be given to the personal-growth aspects of the A.A. experience. Sobriety gradually takes on all the multiple meanings of recovery, of social restoration, of mental and spiritual health. A.A.'s acknowledge this larger meaning of sobriety by employing the contrasting term *dry*—"just being dry"—to refer to the minimum state of not drinking, without any of the other personal changes which spell "real sobriety."

This does not mean that alcoholics who have grown in their sobriety can ever afford to forget that they still have a latent vulnerability which precludes their return to "safe" drinking. They can never afford to forget that the special relationship to drinking can never be totally extinguished. Under future conditions—increased stress, for example—the old relationship to alcohol may again be activated enough to lead to drinking. Also, alcoholics can never forget that if drinking is resumed they have a permanent condition (presumed by most A.A.'s to be physiological in nature) which will make them unable, for long, to control the extent of their drinking—thus initiating a repetition of the old, disastrous alcoholic pattern.

In this dual sense, "powerlessness over alcohol" is never to be forgotten. But the *main thrust* of the A.A. program, as the member moves along, is not upon staying away from alcohol but upon *learning to live*. Alcohol is mentioned only once in the Twelve Steps. Almost all of the Twelve Steps program— and most of the interpersonal interaction and group dynamics in the A.A. society—have to do with learning a satisfying, fulfilling way of life, one which builds or rebuilds self-esteem, cultivates productive relationships with other persons, and gives meaning and worth to one's existence.

Becoming able to stay away from drinking is the foremost concern at first. But after a while, there comes the happy, and for some surprising, discovery that A.A. has much more than that to give:

When I first came to A.A., before I started getting comfortable, I would make three or four meetings a week, and sometimes not even that many. Now, after I found out what A.A. has to offer, I make between seven and eight meetings a week. (28-M-0/5)

At first, some A.A.'s view the process of learning the new way of life as primarily a conscious, mental process. Some of it is. As Yalom (pp. 3–44) points out, intellectual understanding does contribute to the change process. But he also makes clear that the personal changes occurring in group therapy are not primarily the product of intellectual processes but of *emotional experiences with other persons*.

One A.A. member, in the program over two years, told of cutting his meeting attendance down, at one stage, from six to three meetings a week "because I thought I could *absorb* more from fewer meetings." He added "But, I know now that I was wrong." Accordingly, he stepped up his meeting attendance, having learned that more change came out of more social interaction.

In my estimation, some thought and individual effort are required, but the acquisition of the new way of life is, above all else, a social process—an acculturation process—much of which is not a conscious process at all. Furthermore, the learning process, the acquisition of the A.A. culture, is greatly enhanced by the quality of the social interaction—the unusual understanding and acceptance, the caring, the honest sharing, etc. The A.A. environment is replete with approval and other interpersonal rewards for each small step forward—for each little evidence of learning to live the A.A. way of life.

Even though A.A. members are keenly aware of the importance of attending meetings and becoming involved with others in the A.A. social environment, they nevertheless do tend to perceive the changes which they experience in very personal terms. We have been discussing some of the factors and processes making for personal change. Let us now turn to a range of personal reports which describe the character of the changes.

An overall, basic change to be noted at the outset is the change in the perception and meaning of both sobriety and A.A. itself:

Initially, I went to A.A. because I really wanted to be a sober person. That's all I wanted. That went on for some time until I really started to appreciate what the program was all about. For me, now, the A.A. program has very little to do with drinking. It is a way of life—and it is a way that's all right for me. (40-M-3/3)

At first, I thought of A.A. as being sort of an outpatient type of thing—meetings that you went to to stay sober. Now, I think of A.A. as a program of living. The A.A. program and what it teaches is getting ingrained in my life, and I don't think of it as separate from my life anymore. It's wrapped up in just about everything I do: the principles of the program, the things I've learned about my relationships with other people, my relationship to my job, and my relationship to my Higher Power. (38-M-3/2)

I have become much more aware of the depth of the A.A. program as my sobriety has grown. I have many close friends in addition to my sponsor, people I love dearly and won't hesitate to go to if I have a problem. I am more comfortable because I know what my problem is. I'm no longer up-tight about being a nondrinking woman in cocktail-drinking situations. My feelings about myself as a person are greatly changed. When I came to the program, I had not lost out in all the material things as many people had, but *I* was lost. I did not know who, what, or where I was. I found "that person" through this program, and I found that I have a lot of good qualities which I am now willing to accept. I have responsibilities that I can accept now. I still have many things that need to be worked on, but by and large, I am comfortable with *me*, and that is the name of the game as far as I am concerned. (48-F-1/11)

In view of all the distortions of reality which are part and parcel of becoming alcoholic, what more relevant description of sobriety could be formulated than the following?

Sobriety, to me, is the ability to live with a degree of comfort with the conditions as they truly exist—in the world of reality.

This man adds his perspective on the A.A. program after 12 years in A.A.:

Through this program, I have found it easier to determine what is reality and what is daydreams, desires, or things of similar gossamer value. And it is no longer necessary to prove something to somebody—probably to myself. I now have the freedom to be precisely what I am. And I can give the other person complete freedom to accept me on this basis. When I do this, I find it unnecessary to do many of the things I used to do. I believe this program had given me something that I understand, that is simple, and that I am able to apply to my thinking and my attitudes. How well I can do this, on a daily basis, is how I measure my spiritual condition. (54-M-12/0)

Gaining a more realistic perception *of oneself* is brought out by many other members. Here, for example, are a range of such gains voiced in response to the interview question: Since entering A.A., in what ways have your attitudes and values been changed—and your feelings about yourself as a person?

I guess the biggest thing about my attitude is that I've gotten more comfortable with being human. In a certain sense, I have a lot better feeling about myself, and on another level, I have a much more realistic feeling about myself. I'm not into having to be superhuman. And I value people. I value human relationships in real closeness and interdependence in a way that I had to reject totally before I came into the program. I accept myself more, and at the same time I expect more realistic things of myself. I'm much more at peace with myself. I'm not always having to be about, proving something to myself or to other people. I just feel a lot better about myself—lots, lots better. (32-F-0/6)

My attitudes have changed just about 180 degrees since being in A.A. My values have certainly changed dramatically. A.A. has given me a whole new way of life that is just so different than what I was used to. My feelings toward me have changed considerably. I didn't have too high a regard for myself when I was drinking. I would say that A.A. has helped me to come to grips with who I am, and has helped me to accept me as I am today, and has helped me discover that I have a few things going for me that I can build on—and hope to continue to build on. (44-M-1/3)

I am a calmer person since coming into A.A. I can cope with everyday problems and situations without picking up a drink.

Things don't bother me as much as they used to. My feelings about myself have changed. I like myself, respect myself, and know that basically I am a good person. (32-F-0/6)

Some of the members interviewed described the learning process in A.A. as one of *growing up*—learning to face life in a mature fashion:

I'm now in A.A. to enjoy myself. I came in hurting, confused, and needing it. The difference now is that I want it, I love it, I enjoy it. My attitude is not fixed. I've become a flexible, open-minded person, less fearful, just a generally more confortable, outgoing type of individual. My values have changed considerably. I've grown up in A.A. I had a very low opinion of myself when I came to A.A. Today, my view of myself is altered 85 percent. I like myself. I accept my alcoholism, just like I accept my green eyes. I feel that I am a well-adjusted person, reasonably happy most of the time. (44-F-2/11)

I used to think of any misfortune or difficulty as just a bad deal, something that shouldn't be. As soon as I became anxious, frustrated, or depressed, I'd drink. There was a whole gamut of emotions I never allowed myself to experience—and as a result, I never grew emotionally. I realize now that frustrating things are not punishment. They are a part of life. They are a part of growth—valuable experiences. (38-M-3/2)

Before A.A., my values were a beautiful home, a beautiful car, a wonderful husband, etc. Today, money things aren't as important. It is important that I am content with me and can live with me. Before, I hated myself—was the worst person on earth—nobody liked me. Then, a year or a year and a half in the program, I stopped running. I think that I had just been running away from me and that I just never grew up. Coming off the pills and the alcohol, it was hard. You come out of it, you're 28 or 29, and you've got to grow up. So there were a lot of growing pains. But, through the growing pains and the changing, and through the Steps, I got to know me—and I got to like me. Today, there is still a lot of work to do, but I don't run away from me anymore. (32-F-4/0)

As attitudes toward oneself are improved, attitudes toward *other persons* are changed for the better as well:

> I like myself for the first time in my life. A.A. has given me the feeling that I have always wanted: to feel free to be me. Now I am. I can accept myself now and that is something I was never able to do in my whole life. And because my attitudes toward me have altered so much, they have altered tremendously toward everyone. (42-F-3/9)

> I naturally thought, at first, that the A.A. program was a selfish program, and so I used it for myself. However, I've learned since that it's more important to help other people. The material things in life have gone way down in value. It is much more important to me to see a person smile or to find an opportunity to help someone else. As for feelings about myself as a person, I certainly understand myself—and life—a whole lot better than I did before. (56-M-5/9)

Breaking out of one's defensive, egocentric shell and becoming interested in, and involved in, the well-being of other persons is probably the most significant, observable change in orientation which occurs when a person "begins to get the program." This change does not come all at once. It is a growth process—never complete—but the direction of change is clear:

> I not only feel that I got back much of what I had lost, but I feel that I am growing inside. And I feel a sense of joyous adventure. I listen much better now. I accept other people better for what they are. This carries over into my whole life—to people outside of A.A. as well. I feel more when people are hurting. I find myself becoming much more open to others. It's more than tolerance—it is more of an acceptance of other human beings. My relationship with my family and community has got increasingly better. I am becoming real—not fragmented, not phoney, but real. (43-M-1/4)

Both the *outer* and *inner* aspects of the changes are brought out in the above—as they are in the following:

My life has completely changed—my own personal life, my relationship with my family and with other people. Inwardly is where I have changed the most. I have more confidence in myself, and I am more at ease. I didn't know what peace of mind or serenity was until I found my own Higher Power and know that I don't have to carry any load alone [don't have to cope with nothing more than the old restricted self]. It is a beautiful life, and I am sorry that it took me 50 years to find it. (50-F-1/4)

In this chapter, I have presented the outlook on self, others, and life which is the essence of the A.A. culture carried by, and learned in, the A.A. society. Of course, the learning and growing is often faltering, is usually slow, and can never be complete. But this is what goes on in the A.A. social environment. It is learning and growing through honest sharing, through entering into each other's lives, through trying to understand and practice the program—trying again and again, each time a little more. It is through associating intimately with others who have been in the same boat and who are also trying to move in the same direction that the new way of life gradually becomes one's own.

For another good, overall description of the desired A.A. results, we have a woman's response after 3 years in A.A.:

I'm no longer the scared, frightened, noncommunicative woman that I was—not the "little girl" that I was—when I came to A.A. I have self-confidence, and I am no longer afraid to help people and to put out my hand and seek to understand them instead of constantly seeking their understanding of me. It is all so different. My attitude is certainly more positive. It is a joy to get up in the morning. The world is no longer a shambles, and it is good to be alive. People are more important to me now, material things less so. It is good to have friends—sure feels good and is wonderful. I still have problems in life, but I don't say I have trouble. Trouble has gone out of my life, and that is great. Trouble no longer rides with me; problems, we all have. (33-F-3/0)

If we view the A.A. program as merely an alcoholism treatment or recovery program, we do not see all that A.A. has to offer—namely, a quality of warm, honest, open, close relationships and a very satisfying new way of living. It is a society and a culture in which the early focus on not drinking gives way to a major focus on living. Personal growth in the A.A. way of life becomes attractive in its own right. Here is the perspective of a woman who was still attending two or three A.A. meetings a week after 21 years:

A.A. gave me a whole new way of life, so I am still continuing on with the things that A.A. taught me—this philosophy I found in A.A. I still apply it daily as I go along. *I feel that I'm still growing.* I've found in A.A. what I think I was looking for in the bottle. I now have a positive outlook on life, and I understand myself. I can recognize my limitations, but I have respect for myself, and I'm much happier. (63-F-21/6)

This is the sobriety which is more than sobriety.

TEN
How They Hang Together

Our focus up to this point has been on the A.A. recovery program. The emphasis has been on the dynamic factors in the A.A. program and social environment which function to reorient alcoholics to themselves, to others, and to life in general.

If those who work with alcoholics also have some familiarity with A.A. customs and modes of operation, they can be more comfortable and surefooted in their referrals to A.A. and in their general relations with local groups and the larger fellowship. This means an acquaintance with A.A.'s *Traditions* and service structure by which over 30,000 groups in the United States and Canada (and about 20,000 groups in other countries) manage to hang together and keep their activities focused on their primary recovery purpose.

In the opening chapter, I quoted Matthew Dumont as observing that A.A. is a distinctively American phenomenon with its emphasis on self-help and pragmatism. The closer one looks at A.A. history, the more one is impressed with how much the development of everything about A.A. emerged from a pragmatic stance—from a willingness to learn from their own experience, extracting and keeping that which "worked." This was true of A.A.'s recovery program. And it was also true of A.A.'s group, intergroup, and fellowshipwide patterns of operation—and of A.A.'s relationships with the larger non-A.A. society.

As stated earlier, cofounder Bill's own experience had shown him that his most effective defense against drinking, when the compulsion was strong, was becoming involved in helping another alcoholic. It was the application of this experience which, after a disappointing business setback in Akron, led him to an alcoholic physician, Dr. Bob.[1]

Together, they began working with other alcoholics. After Bill returned to New York, each continued to devote much time to such effort and involvement. It kept them sober. However, they had much more failure than success with others. In fact, after 18 months (at the end of 1936), the sober members of the Akron and New York clusters added up to the grand total of only 10, including Dr. Bob and Bill. They still had much to learn.

From the beginning, the Akron and New York contingents had operated in the context of the Oxford Groups (Russell 1932). When, however, Bill and a few of the New York alcoholics followed their Oxford Group meetings with informal get-togethers by themselves, they discovered something important. Here, by themselves, they felt less inhibited, better understood, and could talk freely about their experiences with their *drinking* problem. They found that they had so much

[1] Accounts of this meeting of A.A.'s cofounders in 1935 and subsequent developments are to be found in A.A.'s own books, *Alcoholics Anonymous Comes of Age* and *Dr. Bob and the Good Oldtimers*; and in Kurtz, *Not-God: A History of Alcoholics Anonymous*.

more to share—and could share more deeply—than was possible in the Oxford Group meetings. Here, by themselves, they were among their own kind. They could identify with each other. And as the details of their life stories were revealed, each saw himself more clearly: not only the long, lonely struggles and defeats of the past, but all the nuances of thought and feeling which were a part of striving for a sober new footing in the present. An indescribable bond developed among them which was amazingly conducive to their own change and growth. They also discovered that this type of setting and atmosphere was much more appealing to the alcoholics they were trying to reach and help. Thus another nuclear element of the A.A. program had come into awareness.

The main roots of their new lives were still in the practices and beliefs of the Oxford Groups whose meetings they continued to attend. But by also meeting separately, afterwards, the values of doing so gradually became so clear that separation from the Oxford Group movement became "thinkable." By 1937, Bill and his fellow New York alcoholics did separate and step out on their own. Two years later, the Akron and Cleveland groups did the same.

Both in and outside the Oxford Groups, the New York and Ohio alcoholics had been accumulating a variety of trial and error experience. They had learned more about themselves and their drinking problems. They had learned the value of involvement in helping each other. They had experienced the many advantages of meeting by themselves. And importantly, they had learned more about how, and how not, to approach the various kinds of alcoholic persons they were trying to help. They were becoming more skillful in penetrating the shells of rationalization and denial, so that during 1937, the total number of sober members grew from 10 to 40.

Still learning, they were nevertheless becoming more confident about their methods. By the end of another year, and after much discussion among themselves, they had become suffi- ciently clear about the ingredients of their approach to put them in writing. Accordingly, Bill began the process of writing a book which pulled together their collective experience regarding both recovery and the more appealing and effective ways of reaching and helping fellow alcoholics. The book was also to include the alcoholism and recovery stories of Bill, Dr. Bob, and, as it turned out, the stories of 28 others out of a total of about 100 who were then sober. Having sometimes called themselves "a nameless bunch of drunks," they finally settled on a title for the book which also gave the groups a name: *Alcoholics Anonymous*.

If anything was ever done on a financial shoestring, it was the publishing of this book. Nevertheless, it saw daylight in April, 1939. Slowly, word about it—and the *almost unbeliev- able* evidence of individual recoveries of "hopeless drunks"— began to circulate, mostly by word of mouth, but assisted by a *Liberty* magazine article (Sept. 1939), a series in the Cleveland *Plain Dealer* (Fall, 1939), and a favorable review by the then best-known clergyman in the United States, Harry Emerson Fosdick. So, by late 1940, about 18 months after the book emerged, Bill could count 22 small groups in the cities of 14 states and the District of Columbia.

For the most part, however, the public was still unaware of the fledgling fellowship. Then in March, 1941, the story of A.A. was told to the nation in the widely read *Saturday Evening Post* in an insightful and compelling article by one of its editors, Jack Alexander. With this, A.A. was launched on the national scene.

A.A. now entered a period of rapid growth. Four years later, in 1945, Bill in his small New York office was aware of about 550 groups with about 15,000 members in the United States. A.A. had also crossed the border into Canada which then had a dozen or so groups with about 250 members.

This growth, however, also spawned new problems. Earlier,

when there were fewer groups, a chain of personal relationships had bound all the groups together. Members of older groups, often traveling business men, helped new groups get started. By word of mouth, they also transmitted what their experience had taught them about how to conduct their group life—principles and practices which not only helped them to hang together but also fostered a favorable group climate for personal recovery.

Now however, with rapid growth, many new groups were unaware of this experience. They were struggling along, alone, improvising their own group patterns. It is not surprising that many of the old mistakes were repeated by some group or another, by this or that individual. Some power-driven or prestige-seeking "leaders" exploited their groups—or their A.A. affiliation. Some went ego-tripping in newspaper headlines. Some copied familiar patterns of other organizations which were not appropriate for A.A. purposes. Some groups set up exclusive membership rules. Sometimes money and property and organizational difficulties disrupted groups. So did questions of leadership, authority, and power. Some personal and jurisdictional rivalries developed. Some groups fell apart. I was told of one early group which got into a hassle with the result that all nine members went out and got drunk. In short, there were all kinds of deviations from the most functional patterns, deviations which not only diluted the recovery atmosphere within given groups, but also threatened the immediate and ultimate welfare of A.A. as a whole.

How were these problems to be met? How could the hard-won experience be made available to all groups? Knowing that individual alcoholics and A.A. groups did not relish being told what to do, and having already become committed to the ideal of peer-group democracy and group autonomy, there could be *no imposition* of what had already been learned about the most functional relationships of members within their groups—or of group relationships with other A.A. groups to A.A. as a whole, and with the world outside. The communication of that which experience had taught them had to be shared *as among equals*. After much discussion, Bill was asked to undertake the task. This he did in a series of articles in the *A.A. Grapevine* in 1946, boldly referring to the principles and practices as "Traditions."

Much of their essence is to be found in the following excerpt from Bill's introduction to the series:

> If, as A.A. members, we can each refuse public prestige and renounce any desire for personal power; if as a movement, we insist on remaining poor, so avoiding disputes about extensive property and its management; if we steadfastly decline all political, sectarian, or other alliances, we shall avoid internal division and public notoriety; if as a movement, we remain a spiritual entity concerned only with carrying our message to fellow sufferers without charge or obligation; then only can we most effectively complete our mission. . . . Unity is so vital to us A.A.'s that we cannot risk those attitudes and practices which have sometimes demoralized other forms of human society. . . .
>
> But A.A. unity cannot automatically preserve itself. Like personal recovery, we shall always have to work to maintain it. Here, too, we surely need honesty, humility, open-mindedness, unselfishness, and, above all—vigilance. So we who are older in A.A. beg you who are newer to ponder the experience we have already had of trying to work and live together. (*A.A. Tradition, How it Developed*, 1955, p. 4)

Now known as The Twelve Traditions, these guiding principles gained increasing attention and acceptance after their first publication. After several years, they were officially adopted at A.A.'s first International Convention, held in Cleveland on the occasion of A.A.'s fifteenth anniversary. The Traditions were introduced by the simple phrase: "Our A.A. experience has taught us that." In their later short form, they are as follows:

THE TWELVE TRADITIONS[2]

1. Our common welfare should come first; personal recovery depends upon A.A. unity.
2. For our group purposes there is but one ultimate authority—a loving God as he may express Himself in our group conscience. Our leaders are but trusted servants; they do not govern.
3. The only requirement for A.A. memership is a desire to stop drinking.
4. Each group should be autonomous except in matters affecting other groups or A.A. as a whole.
5. Each group has but one primary purpose—to carry its message to the alcoholic who still suffers.
6. An A.A. group ought never endorse, finance or lend the A.A. name to any related facility or outside enterprise, lest problems of money, property, and prestige divert us from our primary purpose.
7. Every A.A. group ought to be fully self-supporting, declining outside contributions.
8. Alcoholics Anonymous should remain forever nonprofessional, but our service centers may employ special workers.
9. A.A., as such, ought never be organized; but we may create service boards or committees directly responsible to those they serve.
10. Alcoholics Anonymous has no opinion on outside issues; hence the A.A. name ought never be drawn into public controversy.
11. Our public relations policy is based on attraction rather than promotion; we need always maintain personal anonymity at the level of press, radio, and films.

---

[2] *Alcoholics Anonymous.* The above and excerpts from the long form are reprinted by permission of A.A. World Services, Inc.

12. Anonymity is the spiritual foundation of all our Traditions, ever reminding us to place principles before personalities.

The original "long form" of the Twelve Traditions[3] is more complete and explicit, containing some points and emphases which are a vital part of the principles and practices generally observed through A.A.

For example, the *open-membership*-for-alcoholics intent of Tradition Three ("The only requirement for membership is a desire to stop drinking") is made very clear in the long form: "Our membership ought to include all who suffer alcoholism. Hence we may refuse none who wish to recover. Nor ought A.A. membership ever depend upon money or conformity." This means no dues or fees (just voluntary contributions) and no exclusion because of status or lifestyle or any other criterion for membership; nothing but a desire to do something about the drinking problem.

Next, we should note the Traditions which serve to protect A.A. groups from common kinds of organizational tendencies which might dilute the group's attention to its primary purpose of personal recovery and helping other alcoholics to recover.

One such major principle (Tradition Seven) is the policy of *total self-support*—not only at the local group level but throughout the fellowship. Outside contributions are not to be sought and are declined if offered, even to the point of diplomatically declining memorial contributions given by the grateful family of a deceased member. This policy gives *individual members* self-respect, and it gives *local groups* and the *total fellowship* a valuable freedom and independence.

The long form of Tradition Nine speaks to the matter of local group organization: "Each A.A. group needs the least possible organization." It also adds the principle of "rotating leadership" (rotation in office), a principle which is almost universal-

---

[3] Found in *A.A. Tradition, How it Developed*; in *Alcoholics Anonymous* 3rd edition; and in *Twelve Steps and Twelve Traditions*.

ly observed at all organizational levels. The advantages of rotation stand out when we recall how often organizations suffer when persons cling too long to the prestige and power of office.

And how often individuals try to increase their influences in an organization by making sizeable contributions. A.A. even has a policy on this: a limit of $500 annually may be accepted from any one member—and the same limit to a bequest from a member, acceptable only in the year of the member's death.

Related to A.A. philosophy of leadership, as stated in Tradition Two (Tradition Nine in the long form): "Our leaders are but trusted servants; they do not govern."

These several Traditions serve to protect A.A. groups and the fellowship as a whole from the liabilities which so frequently plague and reduce the effectiveness of many other organizations. They serve to counter the common tendencies to forget that money, property, organization, and leadership are only *means* and that means find their most functional place only when the *ends* are kept clearly in view—which in A.A. is recovery from alcoholism.

Another tradition (Eight) is directed to individuals in A.A., stressing the point that "A.A. should remain forever nonprofessional" in the sense that, as the long form states, "our usual Twelfth Step work is never to be paid for." This reinforces the recovery point that the giving of oneself "without stint, with no demand for reward" is a central ingredient of the individual member's own recovery.[4]

---

[4] This Tradition does not bar individual A.A. members from becoming employed in the alcoholism field, but individuals should not be employed as A.A. members, or identified as such. A.A.'s who work in the field will find much helpful guidance in the experiences shared in one of the *A.A. Guidelines*: "For A.A. Members Employed in the Alcoholism Field." This publication is addressed to A.A. members, not to employing agencies. But the directors and staffs of the latter will be enabled to look at the total situation through A.A. eyes, thus clarifying roles. Available from the General Service Office.

Because Tradition Six is so relevant to A.A.'s stance with regard to all non-A.A. programs, agencies, and persons professionally dealing with alcoholics, I wish to quote the original long-form version in full:

Tradition Six: Problems of money, property, and authority may easily divert us from our primary spiritual aim. We think, therefore, that any considerable property of genuine use to A.A. should be separately incorporated and managed, thus dividing the material from the spiritual. An A.A. group, as such, should never go into business. Secondary aids to A.A., such as clubs or hospitals which require much property or administration, ought to be incorporated and so set apart that, if necessary, they can be freely discarded by the groups. Hence such facilities ought not to use the A.A. name. Their management should be the sole responsibility of those people who financially support them. For clubs, A.A. members are usually preferred. But, hospitals, as well as other places of recuperation, ought to be well outside A.A.—and medically supervised. While an A.A. group may cooperate with anyone, such cooperation ought never go so far as affiliation or endorsement, actual or implied. An A.A. group can bind itself to no one.

In this Tradition, we find the basis for the phrase "cooperation but not affiliation," which continues to guide A.A. Despite the minority of members who perceive almost any cooperation as affiliation, the trend throughout A.A. has definitely been toward more cooperative interaction with the professional community. In a changing world, with so much more non-A.A. alcoholism activity, more ways of cooperating have been found to be not only compatible but desirable. Experience, however, has indicated that A.A. makes a stronger and more helpful resource if it retains its complete independence. "No affiliation" has proven to be a sound, functional policy.

Traditions Ten and Eleven deal with the relations of A.A.

groups and members to the society surrounding them. It was clear from their own early experience that their attention to their primary purpose could easily be endangered by becoming involved in "outside controversial issues—particularly those of politics, alcohol reform, or sectarian religion . . . and that therefore . . . No A.A. group or member should ever, in such a way as to implicate A.A., express any opinion on outside controversial issues. . . . The A.A. groups oppose no one."

A.A.'s so-called Preamble (opposite page 1) sums it up well: "A.A. is not allied with any sect, denomination, politics, organization, or institution; does not wish to engage in any controversy, neither endorses nor opposes any causes. Our primary purpose is to stay sober and help other alcoholics to achieve sobriety."

Tradition Eleven, the so-called Anonymity Tradition, really has two parts. The first is: "Our public relations policy is based on attraction rather than promotion." As elaborated in the long form: "We think A.A. ought to avoid sensational advertising. . . . There is never need to praise ourselves. We feel it is better to let our friends recommend us." This sounds strange in our contemporary world, but the practice of this policy has made many friends, including members of the press. I believe this has been and continues to be a productive policy.

The anonymity part reads: "We need always maintain personal anonymity at the level of press, radio and films." This means all public media of communication, including articles and books. This is what is referred to as the *Anonymity Tradition* as distinguished from anonymity in general. For perspective, let us consider the multiple values of anonymity.

Originally, being anonymous was a simple response to the prevailing stigma. It protected members from public identification as alcoholics, and it promised the same protection to those considering coming to A.A. This much is easy to understand: A.A. would not have grown or even survived without it. The stigma has been lessened today, but it is still quite strong so that the practice and promise of anonymity are still of vital importance from this point of view.

As for anonymity at the personal level, individual members are free—in fact encouraged—to reveal their own A.A. membership to family members, close friends, their doctors, and clergymen. However, there is a strong taboo against revealing the A.A. affiliation of *any other member* to *anyone* outside A.A. without that member's permission. As Bill once wrote, "It should be the privilege of each A.A. member to cloak himself with as much personal anonymity as he desires. His fellow A.A.'s should respect his wishes" (*The A.A. Tradition: How it Developed* pp. 37–38). As a corollary, it is also understood among A.A. members that personal revelations made in A.A. meetings are to be treated as confidential—not repeated outside the meeting.

In an anonymous, confidential setting, members are much more free to work the recovery program. Honest catharsis and utter frankness become safe. Members are insulated from what their former associates might think and are thereby freed to look at themselves afresh and begin trying out the new ways of thinking and relating to people. They may slip or stumble without being misunderstood. They are free to consider and cultivate the whole range of new attitudes and values inherent in the A.A. philosophy and orientation to life. The members are in a new reference group and are liberated by anonymity and confidentiality from the gaze and opinions of their outside friends and colleagues.

With regard to the Tradition of anonymity at the public media level, we should note that this Tradition has had, and continues to have, great protective value for A.A. as a whole. Without it, A.A. would not have come into its present strength and unity. And today, its general acceptance within the fellowship puts a brake on those members whose drive for recognition, power, or personal gain tempts them to exploit their A.A. affiliation. The Tradition also puts a brake on those members who, in effect, seek to marry the name of A.A. to enterprises or causes of one sort or another. There have been and there continue to be some who seek publicity as A.A. members or seek to become self-appointed spokesmen for A.A.[5]

A corollary of the Tradition is that no individual member is ever to be recognized as a spokesman for A.A. Each member speaks for himself, not for A.A. as a whole. How deeply this is embedded among A.A. members is reflected in the frequency with which one hears members say, "I can't speak for A.A.; what I have to say is my own opinion."

Granted the protective value to A.A. of anonymity at the public media level, does A.A.'s policy nevertheless have the new effect, as a few critics have charged, of perpetuating the stigma attached to alcoholism? I think not. As a long-time student of, and participant in, the alcoholism movement, I believe that by repeatedly demonstrating the reality of recovery, A.A. has done more to reduce the stigma of alcoholism in the public mind than anything which has happened in our time.

As for the future, it is my judgment that A.A. will continue to serve the stigma-reducing goal best not by dropping its tradition of anonymity at the media level, but by continuing its undistracted focus on its recovery program—upon being A.A. at its recovery/reorientation best. As long as there is even a tiny percentage of prestige-hungry or power-driven persons in A.A., the policy of anonymity at the public media level will continue to be best not only for A.A. but for the whole alcoholism movement—best serving the desired goal of stigma reduction.

The Twelfth and last Tradition reads: "Anonymity is the spiritual foundation of all our traditions, ever reminding us to place principles before personalities." This is further clarified

---

[5] An instructive review of the actual experiences out of which the Anonymity Tradition emerged is to be found in *Alcoholics Anonymous Comes of Age*, pp. 128–137.

in the long form which adds "that we are actually to practice genuine humility." That means a nondefensive, nonegocentric, non-self-serving orientation to oneself, others, and life in general—an orientation which, we remind ourselves, indicates the direction of growth and not a state ever fully achieved.

So we see that in A.A., anonymity has accrued to itself all the meanings of *confidentiality* and *humility*—and that, in this sense, anonymity is the nonegocentric "spiritual foundation of all our traditions." This orientation is as basic to the Traditions as we have seen it to be in the recovery program.

Such, then, are the Twelve Traditions which grew out of A.A.'s collective experience. Even though individuals—and groups—will at times deviate from these guiding principles and practices, the Twelve Traditions are as much a part of A.A. as the Twelve Steps. When groups get into trouble of one kind or another, they can find their way again by a restudy of the experience and wisdom summed up in the Traditions. And because the Traditions are in certain respects quite different from the customs and operations of most organizations and agencies in our society, non-A.A. workers with alcoholics will find it useful to be aware of them—to recognize their value not merely in terms of A.A.'s viability but also in terms of A.A.'s recovery effectiveness—and to take them into account when working with or relating to A.A.

In addition to the Traditions, A.A. has a structure by which A.A.'s collective work is carried on and its decisions made.

At the local metropolitan level, this means a Central Office, often called the Intergroup Office, which provides information, receives and channels referrals to local groups, publishes a listing of local meetings, indicating time and place and whether open or closed, and perhaps also publishes a newsletter. Even in small communities with only a group or two, there will be an A.A. number listed in the phone directory.

A.A. in the United States and Canada also has an overall office located in New York. Called the General Service Office

(G.S.O.), its scope is to serve all groups and A.A. as a whole. This it does in ways too numerous to list. But briefly, it implements the work of specialized trustee's committees dealing with such matters as public information, cooperation with the professional community, working with treatment facilities and correctional facilities, new literature, the annual conference (see below), etc. G.S.O. also has the very important function of publishing and distributing A.A.'s own books and abundant literature.[6]

As for groups in other countries, it has been A.A.'s policy to encourage the establishment of their own national service offices. By 1982, there were 19 such national or zonal offices. G.S.O. in New York continues direct service to groups in countries without such a service center.

The General Service Office and all its publishing activities are managed by a nonprofit corporation, A.A. World Services, Inc., which has its own working directors but is wholly owned by A.A.'s top legal body, the General Service Board. This board of trustees also owns the separate corporation which publishes A.A.'s official monthly magazine, the *A.A. Grapevine*.

We should also note the way in which A.A. groups are tied in with the process of making policy for the conduct of A.A.'s fellowshipwide affairs.

During A.A.'s early years, the cofounders exercised the most influence and were the chief link between the groups and the operation of so called headquarters. But when Dr. Bob lay seriously ill (he died in late 1950), reminding Bill of his own mortality, serious thought was given to devising a structure through which the fellowship itself could take over from the founders and successfully direct its collective affairs.

The result, spelled out in great detail in the *A.A. Service*

[6] The General Service Office mailing address is: P.O. Box 459, Grand Central Station, New York, NY 10163. Its location is at 468 Park Avenue South.

Manual, becomes most visible each April in the week-long General Service Conference, meeting in New York. This body is unique in several ways.

The voting membership of the Conference consists not only of area delegates (from 91 U.S. and Canadian geographic areas) but also of persons actively involved in carrying on A.A.'s fellowshipwide affairs, namely, the trustees of the General Service Board, the directors of the two corporations (A.A. World Services, Inc., and *A.A. Grapevine*, Inc.), and A.A. staff members of the General Service Office and the *Grapevine* office. Area delegates are always to constitute at least two-thirds of the Conference members. But "voting power" is not really an issue because the purpose of the Conference is to pool experience and develop an informed consensus: "advisory actions." Furthermore, the Conference operates on the general principle that no position or policy is to become an advisory action until there is *substantial unanimity*.

Lacking that, the matter will receive further consideration or postponement until greater agreement is reached. But once arrived at, advisory actions are taken seriously. They are thought of as representing the "group conscience" of the fellowship as a whole (subject, however to revision at a later Conference).

Begun on a trial basis in 1951, the Conference plan was adopted in 1955 by the 20th Anniversay International Convention and has been working well ever since.

In effect, the establishment of the General Service Conference structure rounded out A.A.'s three major components, called "The Three Legacies"—the recovery program, the guiding Traditions, and third, the General Service Conference and the related general service structure in each of the 91 delegate areas.

With this work done, Bill put into writing the story of the 20-year development in *Alcoholics Anonymous Comes of Age*, published in 1957. This is a very readable, interesting review of the historical experiences and pragmatic reasons for the development of all three components. This book does much to explain why A.A. has taken the shape it has.

Even after having turned over to the fellowship the conduct of its own affairs, Bill nevertheless continued in an active "senior statesman" role. He helped in refining the service structure. He repeatedly reminded one and all of the experiences—and the pragmatic rationale—which led to the fashioning of every aspect of A.A. He also put into writing an exposition of principles and philosophy to provide further clarification, emphasis, and guidance. Called *The Twelve Concepts for World Service*, or simply *The Concepts*, they were adopted by the General Service Conference in 1962.

When I interviewed Bill in his home in 1969, he struck me as a man who had not only had the satisfaction of guiding the development of a unique, mutual-help movement, but had also had the privilege of completing his creative contributions. He had done all he could to prepare the fellowship for a future of remarkable strength.

What Bill, Dr. Bob, and some key others helped to design is, as I noted earlier, different in many ways. Nevertheless, I suggest that A.A.'s effectiveness and survival lie in these very differences. In a society characterized by competitive striving for status, recognition, power, and their material symbols, A.A. has a recovery program based upon opposite values— upon learning a nonegocentric way of life. Furthermore, A.A. has a collective life—traditions and structure—which is remarkably congruent with, and supportive of, the basic recovery program. There is no confusion of ends and means. There is singleness of purpose. There is an internal harmony of program, principles and practices which stands in striking contrast to the operations of most organizations and agencies in our society. Even though individuals and groups in A.A. often fall short of the mark, and while it is equally true that no social organization is immune from drift and foundering, it appears to me that A.A. is provided with some unusual assets for keeping itself on course in the forseeable future.

ELEVEN
On Working with A.A.

In a lecture comment, I heard Robert Coles make the point that his primary goal in writing the *Children in Crisis* books had been not just understanding but *awareness*—reader awareness of the actual settings and experiences of the children studied.

The distinction fascinated me. After all, there are multiple ways of conceptualizing the same human dynamics. The problem with our respective understandings is that they often become discipline-restricted or ideology-bound. Awareness cannot, of course, totally correct this limitation, but it does free us to come closer to the phenomena we are trying to understand.

Reader awareness of the many facets of A.A. experience has been my goal as well. True, I have shared my own understandings. But I hope I have included enough "awareness description" of A.A. phenomena and personal A.A. experience material to let readers apply their own understandings.

Nevertheless, as stated at the beginning, a book is no substitute for first-hand attendance at A.A. meetings and personally talking to members themselves. This is the next step in awareness and will pay off handsomely. Such personal contacts can add significantly to a professional's competence in successfully referring patients or clients to A.A.—or, for that matter, just add to ease and confidence in talking to them.

Such personal contact and interaction will not only yield a more insightful perception of what goes on in the A.A. environment, but also a greater awareness of what *becoming* alcoholic is like. The latter is basic, for unless we are aware of the interrelated changes which develop in an alcoholic's life during his drinking career, words like "treatment" or even "recovery" will have a certain limiting logic.

There is no substitute for hearing alcoholics describe their own experiences to make us keenly aware of how central and powerful the compulsion to drink can become—to the point where, despite unwanted physiological, psychological, or social consequences, the alcoholic is no longer able to leave alcohol alone, for long, and no longer able consistently to control the amount consumed once drinking is underway.

Furthermore, there is nothing like listening to alcoholics describe their own experiences to make us keenly aware of the other changes which occur in the course of becoming alcoholic. These are the drinking-aggravated changes in behavior patterns, in attitudes and values, and even in the held-to-be-true ideas and "facts" which have to do with alcoholic's self-concept and the way he or she relates to other persons and to life.

Such personal acquaintance will also help us to appreciate the logicalness of the A.A. approach—the logic of coming to grips with the *total, interrelated field*, beginning with the powerlessness over alcohol but also including an overall reorienting of the alcoholic to self, to other persons, and to life in general, in ways which are no longer self-defeating but lead in the direction of emotional health and self-fulfillment.

Personal acquaintance will also make us more fully aware of the potency of the A.A. setting and the manner in which alcoholic newcomers are helped to face, and to cope with, their compulsion to drink; and helped to achieve a highly satisfying way of living without alcohol.

We should never underestimate the reorientating power of the A.A. environment. We may correctly categorize A.A. groups as self-help or mutual-help groups, alcoholics helping each other—helping and being helped. We may also describe A.A. groups as peer-support groups, which they are. But the general usage of these terms still falls short of the A.A. social reality which is more like that of a close-knit family: an intimate, primary group where there is an accumulation of shared experiences, mutual identification, easy give and take, acceptance and unconditional belongingness. Like families, of course, A.A. groups vary considerably in their approximation of these ideal qualities. However, there is generally a remarkable degree of empathy and acceptance—an impressive degree of what A.A.'s sum up by the simple but significant words: *caring* and *sharing*.

If a professional helper is sufficiently aware of what A.A. is and what it can do, a comfortable and productive relationship is possible. I once asked a friend, a psychotherapist in private practice, whether he had any alcoholic clients and, if so, how he worked with them. I was impressed with his reply:

Well, in view of an alcoholic's needs and the best use of my time and skills, my approach is to get my alcoholic clients into A.A., if I can, and then help them make it in A.A. This works with most alcoholics.

Let's say that the client is a woman. I help her prepare for A.A.

by dealing with any sterotypes or anxieties she may have about A.A. I point out A.A.'s effectiveness. I arrange for a personal contact with an A.A. woman member who will take her in hand, accompany her to meetings, and help her become acquainted with other members in the group. I continue appointments with her, but mainly to help her get the most out of being in A.A. If she has a problem with another member, we work on that. If she has trouble with a particular part of the A.A. program, or something said by another member, we work on that. If her group does not appear to be a good fit, I encourage her to visit around and find a group where she can feel more at home. If there is not another group in the community or nearby, I encourage her to associate more with those members in her group whom she does admire. In every way I can, I encourage her to get involved.

The therapist then summed up his perspective on A.A. and working with it:

A.A. is a powerful social environment, not only for helping an alcoholic give up drinking but also for helping an alcoholic grow emotionally. I believe I serve my alcoholic clients best by helping them become involved in that environment and then to derive the most out of their involvement.

I once thought of A.A. as an adjunct to my professional efforts, but I found that alcoholic clients who got involved in A.A. made so much progress that I began to think of A.A. as the primary change agent and to think of my own role as being, for the most part, a supportive one.

This cleared the air for me, and I now feel very comfortable working with clients in this way.[1]

It is important for a hesitant professional to know that it is easy to become acquainted with A.A. in the community. Most

[1] Other professional experience on working with A.A. is to be found in Bean and Zinberg (1981), Curlee (1974), Fox (1973), Groupé (1978), Norris (1978), Vaillant (1983), and Zimberg, Wallace, and Blume (1978). Relevant also is A.A.'s own pamphlet: *A.A. as a Resource for the Medical Profession* (1982).

A.A. members are pleased to have professionals show interest. About all a person needs to do is to let it be known to one or more members that he or she would like to become better acquainted with A.A. and, if possible, to be taken around to a number of open meetings. One way or another, it will be arranged.

We turn now to the greatly increased number of alcoholism treatment places, both residential and outpatient but particularly those which are "A.A.-oriented" and which try to prepare their patients for continuing their recovery in A.A. With a large and growing proportion of newcomers to A.A. now composed of men and women who have treatment-center experience (the majority of newcomers in many places), it is important *how well* the treatment staff members prepare their patients for productively continuing in A.A.

In turn, how well A.A. members and groups receive alcoholics coming from treatment centers is also important. This has been a matter of active concern in A.A. circles and, as I have indicated, is improving. But the improvement is uneven. Some groups and members are further along than others in responding to this changing situation—further along in learning how to sponsor and assimilate newcomers with a treatment-center background.

We may also observe, however, among treatment centers which are A.A.-oriented, that some do a better job than others in preparing their patients for entering A.A. and deriving the most out of their A.A. involvement.

By now, enough experience has been accumulated to point up several areas of difficulty.

One source of difficulty is to be found in the failure of some A.A.-oriented treatment centers to keep a sufficiently sharp distinction between the treatment center and A.A. itself. If, during their stay in the treatment center, the patients have had educational sessions *about* A.A., have attended some A.A.

"meetings" in the center, and may even have taken the first five of A.A.'s Twelve Steps, they may easily come to feel that they are already "in A.A."

Some of them may even believe, when they leave the treatment center (after 28 days or so), that they already know more about A.A. and have progressed further in A.A. than members back home will usually learn or accomplish in a year or two. Obviously, this attitude does not sit well with the A.A. members back home. Moreover, this perception reflects a very limited view of A.A. *Knowing* about the program—or even starting to "work the Twelve Steps" is not being *in* A.A.—not being part of the all-important social process and continuing environment of A.A.

A second source of difficulty is confusion about the role of alcoholism counselors who are also A.A. members.

Today, the staffs of most treatment centers include "alcoholism counselors" who are recovered alcoholics—often A.A. members. If such counselors themselves and the non-A.A. staff members (including persons in management) are not very clear about the difference between being an *A.A. member off the job* and being an *alcoholism counselor on the job*, staff difficulties are bound to ensue. Moreover, without such role clarity, patients are also likely to become confused about A.A. itself.

Having sat in on discussions of the problems faced by A.A. members who are alcoholism counselors, I am acutely aware of the need to keep the two roles separate—not only in each counselor's mind but in *everyone's* mind. This is not an easy matter. However, it is my observation that it is more easily accomplished when such counselors have had three to five years of "good sobriety" in A.A. *before* becoming counselors, and when they have also acquired sufficient special counseling skills to be effective counselors. Recent standards for being a certified alcoholism counselor and the increase in training opportunities for meeting the standards are helping in this regard.[2]

A third difficulty arises when *some* of the treatment centers which treat drug addicts and alcoholics together also encourage all of their drug addicts to go to A.A. after leaving treatment—including drug addicts who have no history of alcohol dependence.

But why not, it may be asked. Why not refer "nonalcoholic addicts" to A.A.? Are not the psychodynamics of drug dependence essentially the same as in alcoholism? Furthermore, if the Twelve Step program is considered to be desirable for drug dependents, then some professionals find it difficulty to understand why A.A. groups should not be wide open to all drug addicts.

What is overlooked in this reasoning is a recognition of the significant fact that A.A. is not just a Twelve Step program, suitable for a variety of problems. The other important component of A.A. is its social environment—a specialized mutual-help society of persons sharing a common background as alcoholics.

The importance of commonalities of problem and experience can be seen more clearly in the case of Gamblers Anonymous which is also based on A.A.'s Twelve Steps. Certainly important in G.A.'s effectiveness is the fact that its groups are composed of compulsive gamblers who can identify with each other in a most compelling way. They speak the same language. They know how a fellow gambler thinks and feels. They have a distinctive, common background of experience which enables them to reach and help each other.

So it is with A.A. It is a nonprofessional mutual-help *society* and *culture* which emerged from the shared experiences of

[2] A helpful sharing of A.A. experience (directed to A.A. members but also informative to non-A.A. members of staff and management) is to be found in *A.A. Guidelines: For A.A. Members Employed in the Alcoholism Field*, available from A.A.'s General Service Office.

becoming and being alcoholic plus the shared experiences of *alcoholics helping alcoholics*. This is the common ground for mutual identification, maximum interaction and group cohesion.

Moreover, it appears to me, that a major reason why the A.A. fellowship has been effective—and continues to be effective—is that it has kept to its primary purpose of being a society of alcoholics helping alcoholics. And A.A. experience to date seems to indicate that this singleness of purpose will continue to be important to A.A. if it's to make its maximum contribution to helping alcoholics in the future.

When we see that the A.A. fellowship is this kind of society, we can understand why A.A. is not able to assimilate *all* types of drug addicts.

Nevertheless it has been demonstrated that A.A. groups *can* assimilate many of those drug addicts who have been sufficiently involved with alcohol to enable them to fit into a group of alcoholics.

It is difficult to determine in advance whether a good fit is possible for a given person. There are many individual factors, and it also depends in part upon the composition of the group. In this regard, it helps to know that many A.A. groups now include some members who have been involved with drugs in addition to alcohol. Consequently, in such groups, there is more freedom to talk about their drug-related experience. The degree of latitude present depends largely upon the composition of a given group; and we should not lose sight of the fact that groups do vary considerably in this respect.

Now, what about "nonalcoholic" drug addicts who cannot fit into A.A. but could fit into an alternative to A.A.? One of the most encouraging recent developments is the resurgence of Narcotics Anonymous, an A.A.-type fellowship for drug addicts. After some years of ups and downs, N.A. is showing stability, now has its own "Big Book" and other literature, and is experiencing rapid growth. N.A. groups are available in almost all urban areas throughout the U.S. and Canada. (N.A. also has groups in a number of other countries.) Treatment professionals and other professional helpers now have a valuable, alternative resource.

What if no N.A. group is available and the only local resource seems to be A.A.? In that case, the patient/client ought to be briefed about A.A. groups and how to relate to them. It would be desirable to point out that A.A. is really a society of alcoholics, but that anyone can attend "open" meetings. And, if there is a choice of open meetings, it may be suggested to select a meeting attended by one or more "dual addicts" who can lend an ear and offer understanding and helpful guidance.

Treatment Center staff members and other professionals interested in preparing their alcoholic patients/clients to get the most out of A.A. should help them understand a number of other things about the A.A. environment and how to derive the greatest benefit from their participation in it.[3]

Patients should know that the A.A. group atmosphere is very nonprofessional. There is no professional structuring. Nor is there confrontational pressure as in some programs. A new A.A. member is not pushed, but is left to travel at his or her own pace. A.A. provides education about the problem and the A.A. way out, not by "teaching" but by the deceptively simple but effective method of sharing experiences. This is even true of its literature. A.A. also provides each person with guides for action in the Twelve Steps and related A.A. literature. And, very important, A.A. provides an interpersonal and group environment of acceptance, warmth, and caring. But, with respect for each person's autonomy, it is essentially up to each individual to find his or her own way.

The prospective member should also be helped to realize

---

[3] The booklet, "Transition from Treatment to A.A.", is filled with experience-based counsel to patients about to leave a treatment setting. Written by Bob W., it is published by Hazelden, 1981.

that deriving the most out the A.A. environment requires *involvement*.

It should be stressed that involvement means more than merely attending meetings, hoping that something will rub off. It means becoming immersed in the A.A. social environment. It means participating in open, honest, sharing and caring interaction with fellow members. Such involvement, of course, does not come all at once. It grows. But it can be made clear to the prospective member that *the degree and quality of involvement with other members will be a major factor in how much will be gained from being in A.A.*

It should also be pointed out that "working the program" includes some *private work* such as reading, studying, taking personal inventory, and cultivating a spiritual realignment.

A prospective member also needs to realize that private work and action with others go hand in hand, each releasing and augmenting the other. The Steps, it can be shown, call for both. For example, a private "searching and moral inventory" of oneself (Step Four) is preparatory to talking it out with another human being (Step Five). Becoming honest with oneself is a necessary private step, but it is the action of bringing this material into the open with another person which brings emotional release and change.

So it is with amends (Step Eight and Nine). The private step of becoming willing to make amends to a person one has harmed is followed by the social act of actually making direct amends. We also note, as pointed out in Step Twelve, that a personal "spiritual awakening" has its expression in the social acts of helping other alcoholics and in practicing "these principles in all our affairs."

In simplest terms, A.A. activity can be described as alcoholics helping, and being helped by, each other. A newcomer's major interest, at first, will be in being helped. But it should be made clear that participation in the A.A. process is not complete until the new member also becomes involved in helping other alcoholics. This is not an add-on duty to the fellowship. Rather, such an outgoing involvement in the progress of someone else is important in the person's *own* recovery—essential for the person's own growth in freedom from constricting egocentricity.

What about the future of professional and A.A. interaction? As documented in the first chapter, present trends are encouraging. We find not only that the proportion of A.A. members utilizing professional help of some kind has steadily increased in recent years, but also that an increasing number of professional persons are recognizing A.A.'s strengths and are learning to work with A.A.

Furthermore, the more experience that professionals have with A.A. the more they are apt to appreciate its nonprofessional characteristics. They come to realize that, both in the present and in the long run, Alcoholics Anonymous can make its greatest overall contribution not by taking on professional ways but by continuing to be an independent, lay, mutual-help society—by continuing to be a very understanding and accepting peer-group fellowship in which alcoholics themselves help each other find the way out of the "world apart" of alcoholism into the freedom of a happier and more satisfying way of life.

Additional Perspective on A.A.

Curlee-Salisbury, Joan. "Perspectives on Alcoholics Anonymous." In Nada J. Estes and M. Edith Heinemann (Eds.), *Alcoholism: Development, Consequences and Interventions*. St. Louis: C. V. Mosby, 1977.

Kurtz, Ernest. *Not-God: A History of Alcoholics Anonymous*. Center City, Minn: Hazelden, 1979.

Madsen, William. "AA: Birds of a Feather." *The American Alcoholic*. C.C. Thomas, Springfield, Il, 1973.

Robinson, David, *Talking Out of Alcoholism: The Self-Help Process of Alcoholics Anonymous*. Baltimore: University Park Press, 1979.

Thune, Carl E., "Alcoholism and the Archetypal Past: A Phenomenological Perspective on Alcoholics Anonymous." *Quarterly Journal of Studies on Alcohol*, 1977, *38*, 75–88.

References

Al-Anon. *Al-Anon Faces Alcoholism* (Rev. ed.). New York: Al-Anon Family Group Headquarters, 1975.

Alcoholics Anonymous. *Alcoholics Anonymous* (3rd ed.). New York: Alcoholics Anonymous World Services, 1976.

Alcoholics Anonymous. *Twelve Steps and Twelve Traditions*. New York: Alcoholics Anonymous World Services, 1953.

Alcoholics Anonymous. *Alcoholics Anonymous Comes of Age: A Brief History of A.A.* New York: Alcoholics Anonymous World Services, 1957.

Alcoholics Anonymous. *Dr. Bob and the Good Oldtimers*. New York: Alcoholics Anonymous World Services, 1980.

Alcoholics Anonymous. *A.A. As a Resource for the Medical Profession*. New York: A.A. World Services, 1983.

Bacon, Selden D. "The Process of Addiction to Alcohol: Social Aspects." *Quarterly Journal of Studies on Alcohol*, 1973, *34*, 1–27.

Bales, R.F. "Cultural Differences in Rates of Alcoholism." *Quarterly Journal of Studies in Alcohol*, 1946, *6*, 480–499.

Bean, Margaret H. "Denial and the Psychological Complications of Alcoholism." In M.H. Bean and N.E. Zinberg (Eds.), *Dynamic Approaches to the Understanding and Treatment of Alcoholism*. New York: The Free Press, 1981.

Bean, Margaret H. and Zinberg, Norman E. (Eds.). *Dynamic Approaches to the Understanding and Treatment of Alcoholism*. New York, The Free Press, 1981.

Bissell, Leclair and Deakins, Susan M. "Smithers Alcoholism Center: A Comprehensive Alcoholism Program in an Urban Voluntary Hospital." In Vincent Groupé (Ed.), *Alcoholism Rehabilitation: Methods and Experiences of Private Rehabilitation Centers*. New Brunswick, N.J.: Rutgers Center of Alcohol Studies, 1978.

Blumberg, Leonard. "The Institutional Phase of the Washingtonian Total Abstinence Movement." *Quarterly Journal of Studies on Alcohol*, 1978, *33*, 1591–1606.

Cahalan, Don. *Problem Drinkers*. San Francisco: Jossey-Bass, 1970.

Caplan, Gerald. *Support Systems and Community Mental Health*. New York: Behavorial Publications, 1974.

Curlee, Joan. "How a Therapist Can Use Alcoholics Anonymous." *Annals of the New York Academy of Sciences*, 1974, *233*, 137–144.

Dumont, Matthew P. "Self-help Treatment Programs." *American Journal of Psychiatry*, 1974, *131*, 631–635.

Fox, Ruth. "Treatment of the Problem Drinker by the Private Practitioner." In P.G. Bourne and R. Fox (Eds.), *Alcoholism: Progress in Research and Treatment*. New York: Academic Press, 1973.

Gantner, Alan and Frank Riessman. *Self-help in the Human Services*. San Francisco: Jossey-Bass, 1977.

Gitlow, Stanley E. "Alcoholism: A Disease." In Peter G. Bourne and Ruth Fox (Eds.), *Alcoholism: Progress in Research and Treatment*. New York: Academic Press, 1973.

Gomberg, Edith Linsansky. "Psychological and Psychosocial Aspects." In Edith Linsansky Gomberg, Helene R. White, and John A. Carpenter (Eds.), *Alcohol, Science and Society Revisited*. University of Michigan Press, Ann Arbor, and Rutgers Center of Alcohol Studies, New Brunswick, N.J., 1982.

Goodwin, Donald W. "Genetic Determinants of Alcoholism." In Jack H. Mendelson and Nancy K. Mello (Eds.), *The Diagnosis & Treatment of Alcoholism*. New York: McGraw-Hill 1979.

Groupé, Vincent (Ed.). *Alcoholism Rehabilitation: Methods and Experiences of Private Rehabilitation Centers*. New Brunswick: Rutgers Center of Alcohol Studies, 1978.

Horney, Karen. *Neurosis and Human Growth*. New York: Norton, 1950.

Hurvitz, Nathan. "Peer Self-help Psychotherapy Groups: Psychotherapy Without Psychotherapists." In Roman, Roman, and Trice (Eds.), *The Sociology of Psychotherapy*. New York: Jason Aronson, 1974.

James, William. *Varieties of Religious Experience*. New York: Modern Library, 1936.

Jellinek, E.M. *The Disease Concept of Alcoholism*. Highland Park, N.J.: Hillhouse Press, 1960.

Johnson, Vernon E. *I'll Quit Tomorrow* (Rev. ed.). New York: Harper & Row, 1980.

Keller, Mark. "The Disease Concept of Alcoholism Revisited." *Quarterly Journal of Studies on Alcohol*, 1976, *37*, 1694–1717.

Keller, Mark and McCormick, Mairi. *Dictionary of Words About Alcohol* (2nd Ed.). New Brunswick: Rutgers Center of Alcohol Studies, 1982.

Kurtz, Ernest. *Not-God: A History of Alcoholics Anonymous*. Center City, Minnesota: Hazelden, 1979.

Lewin, Kurt. *Field Theory in Social Science*. New York: Harper and Row, 1951.

Lewin, Kurt and Grabbe, Paul. "Conduct, Knowledge and Acceptance of New Values." In Kurt Lewin (Ed.), *Resolving Social Conflicts*. New York: Harper and Row, 1948.

Mack, John E. "Alcoholism, A.A., and the Governance of the Self." In Margaret H. Bean and Norman E. Zinberg (Eds.), *Dynamic Approaches to the Understanding and Treatment of Alcoholism*. New York: The Free Press, 1981.

Maxwell, Milton A. *Social Factors in the Alcoholics Anonymous Program*. Unpublished doctoral dissertation, University of Texas, 1949.

Maxwell, Milton A. "The Washingtonian Movement." *Quarterly Journal of Studies on Alcohol*, 1950, *11*, 410–451.

Maxwell, Milton A., Lemere, Frederick, and O'Hollaren, Paul. "Changing Characteristics of Private Hospital Alcoholics: A 20-year Time-trend Analysis." *Quarterly Journal of Studies on Alcohol*, *19*, 309–315, 1958.

Maxwell, Milton A. "Early Identification of Problem Drinkers in Industry." *Quarterly Journal of Studies in Alcohol*, 1960, *21*, 655–678.

Maxwell, Milton A. "Alcoholic Employees: Behavior Changes and Occupational Alcoholism Programs." *Alcoholism*, 1972, *8*, 174–180.

Maxwell, Milton A. "Contemporary Utilization of Professional Help by Alcoholics Anonymous Members." *Annals of N.Y. Academy of Sciences*, 1976, *272*, 436–441.

Norris, John L. "The Role of Alcoholics Anonymous in Rehabilitation." In Vincent Groupe (Ed.), *Alcoholism Rehabilitation: Methods and Experiences of Private Rehabilitation Centers*. New Brunswick: Rutgers Center of Alcohol Studies, 1978.

Pendery, Mary L., Maltzman, Irving M. and West, L. Jolyon. "Controlled Drinking by Alcoholics? New Findings and a Reevaluation of a Major Affirmative Study." *Science*, 1982, *217*, 169–175.

Peterson, W. Jack and Maxwell, Milton A. "The Skid Road 'Wino'." *Social Problems*, 1958, *5*, 308–316.

Robinson, David and Henry, Stuart. *Self-help and Health: Mutual Aid for Modern Problems*. London: Marin Robertson, 1977.

Rogers, Carl. *On Becoming a Person*. Boston: Houghton Mifflin Company, 1961.

Royce, James E. "Causality of Alcoholism." In *Alcohol Problems and Alcoholism*. New York: The Free Press, 1981.

Russell, A.J. *For Sinners Only*. New York: Harper & Brothers, 1932.

Silkworth, William D. "The Doctors Opinion," in Alcoholics Anonymous, *Alcoholics Anonymous*, 3rd ed. pp. xxiii–xxx. A.A. World Services, Inc., New York, 1976.

Sullivan, Harry Stack. *Conceptions of Modern Psychiatry*. Washington: The William Alanson White Psychiatric Foundation, 1945.

Tiebout, Harry M. "The Act of Surrender in the Therapeutic Process." *Quarterly Journal of Studies on Alcohol*, 1949, *10*, 54–55.

Tiebout, Harry M. "Alcoholics Anonymous—An Experiment of Nature." *Quarterly Journal of Studies of Alcohol*, 1961, *22*, 52–68.

Vaillant, George E. "Dangers of Psychotherapy in Treatment of Alcoholism." In Margaret H. Bean and Norman E. Zinberg (Eds.), *Dynamic Approaches to the Understanding and Treatment of Alcoholism*. New York: The Free Press, 1981.

Vaillant, George E. *The Natural History of Alcoholism: Causes, Patterns and Paths to Recovery*. Cambridge, Mass.: Harvard University Press, 1983.

W., Bill. *A.A. Tradition: How It Developed*. New York: Alcoholics Anonymous World Services, 1955.

W., Bob. *Transition from Treatment to A.A.* Center City, Minn.: Hazelden, 1981.

Wallace, John. "Alcoholism From the Inside out: A Phenomenological Analysis." In Nada J. Estes and M. Edith Heinemann (Eds.), *Alcoholism: Development, Consequences, and Interventions* (2nd ed.). St. Louis: Mosby, 1982.

White, Helene Raskin. "Sociological Theories of the Etiology of Alcoholism." In Edith L. Gomberg, Helene R. White, and John A. Carpenter (Eds.), *Alcohol, Science and Society Revisited*. University of Michigan Press, Ann Arbor and Rutgers Center of Alcohol Studies, New Brunswick, N.J., 1982.

Yalom, Irvin D. *The Theory and Practice of Group Psychotherapy* (2nd ed.). New York: Basic Books, 1975.

Zimberg, Sheldon, Wallace, John, and Blume, Sheila (Eds.). *Practical Approaches to Alcoholism Psychotherapy*. New York: Plenum, 1978.

Zinberg, Norman E. "Alcohol Addiction: Toward a More Comprehensive Definition." In Margaret H. Bean and N.E. Zinberg (Eds.), *Dynamic Approaches to the Understanding and Treatment of Alcoholism*. New York: The Free Press, 1981.

Zinberg, Norman E. and Bean, Margaret H. "Introduction: Alcohol Use, Alcoholism, and the Problems of Treatment." In Margaret H. Bean and Norman E. Zinberg (Eds.), *Dynamic Approaches to the Understanding and Treatment of Alcoholism*. New York: The Free Press, 1981.

Index

165

ABOUT THE AUTHOR

Milton A. Maxwell, Ph.D., is Professor Emeritus of Sociology, the Center of Alcohol Studies, and former Director of the Summer School of Alcohol Studies at Rutgers University. He has been interested in the social and psychological aspects of the A. A. program since doing his doctorate on that subject. Dr. Maxwell has continued his study of A. A. dynamics, and he has also been a frequent contributor to the literature on alcoholics and alcoholism.

43 field changes